PARACRITICISMS

Seven Speculations of the Times

IHAB HASSAN

University of Illinois Press

URBANA   CHICAGO   LONDON

LIBRARY OF CONGRESS CATALOGING IN PUBLICATION DATA

Hassan, Ihab Habib, 1925–
   Paracriticisms: seven speculations of the times.

   Includes bibliographical references.
   CONTENTS: Frontiers of criticism: 1963, 1969, 1972.
—Postmodernism: a paracritical bibliography.—Joyce-
Beckett: a scenario in 8 scenes and a voice.—(   ):
Finnegans Wake and the postmodern imagination. [etc.]
   1. Literature, Modern—20th century—Addresses,
essays, lectures.   I. Title.
PN771.H34   809'.05   74-19108
ISBN 0-252-00469-8

PARACRITICISMS

The world does not revolve around
those who invent new upheavals but
around those who invent new values;
it revolves in silence.

NIETZSCHE

CONTENTS

Acknowledgments

I should like to thank the Vilas Trust Fund and the University of Wisconsin–Milwaukee for their generous and continued support of my research. The Graduate School has been particularly helpful with its summer grants.

Some pieces in this volume have appeared, in earlier versions, in the following publications:

"Frontiers of Criticism: 1963, 1969, 1972," in *Comparative Literature Studies*, I, no. 4 (Fall, 1964); *Virginia Quarterly*, 46, no. 1 (Winter, 1970); and *Boundary 2*, I, no. 1 (Fall, 1972).

"POSTmodernISM," *New Literary History*, III, no. 1 (Fall, 1971).

"Joyce-Beckett," *Journal of Modern Literature*, I, no. 1 (Spring, 1970).

"Fiction and Future," in Ihab Hassan, ed., *Liberations: New Essays on the Humanities in Revolution* (Middletown, Conn.: Wesleyan University Press, 1971). Copyright Wesleyan University Press.

"The New Gnosticism," *Boundary 2*, I, no. 3 (Spring, 1973).

Some of the ideas and phrases in this work were also tested out in *Arts in Society, Cultural Information Service, Diacritics, Massachusetts Review*, and *Tri-Quarterly*. To all these periodicals I am grateful.

In the last three years, I have been fortunate to have Hans Mayer as a colleague at Wisconsin and as a friend. His vast and joyful knowledge of the humanities, his historical zest, opened new areas for me which I have yet to explore.

There are also acknowledgments too personal for speech: B. H.

Personal Preface

The seven speculations in this work were conceived over the years but share a particular mood: awareness of the age, engagement with certain ideas, certain dreams, love and exasperation mingling in my sense of literature, a desire to break out of criticism. Some of the pieces were occasional; they were delivered as lectures. All were written and rewritten so that, together, they may offer a modest trial of my own discourse.

I am not certain what genre these seven pieces make. I call them paracriticism: essays in language, traces of the times, fictions of the heart. Literature is part of their substance, but their critical edge is only one of many edges in the mind. I would not protest if they were denied the name of criticism. Perhaps I should simply say: in these essays I write neither as critic nor scholar—nor yet impersonate poet, novelist, or playwright—but try to find my voice in the singular forms that speculation sometimes requires. Yet what, finally, is singular? Every voice is cursed by its echo, blessed by an answer this side of mortality.

These paracriticisms stand, I hope, in some active relation to one another; they compose a sequence. The earlier concern broad issues of literary criticism; the latter pertain to general questions of culture and consciousness. In the middle, the focus narrows on literature, on Joyce and Beckett particularly, who contain the extreme tensions of the contemporary imagination. Indeed, the focus narrows still more on *Finnegans Wake*, which raises the same questions with which the work ends and begins.

I do not claim for these essays the logic of a sustained exposition, as I do not disclaim their deliberate relations. They were meant to come together in an order which assumes provisional disconfirmation, discontinuity, silence, space, and surprise. Still, familiar devices abound in the work: typographic variation and thematic repetition, serialism and its parody, allusion and analogy, query and collage, quotation and juxtaposition; these paracritical essays, I fear, do not disconfirm enough. Their effect, at any rate, is scarcely new, except in academic criticism. Yet even academic critics may learn, say, from *The Waste Land* or *The Cantos* what neither Eliot nor Pound would have cared to teach. For the issue is not one of criticism imitating art; it is rather one of writers using the resonances of their voices, the values of their lives.

Still, I suspect that the literary act is more gratuitous, its frames more contingent, than we like to admit. These frames—historical, philosophic, social, personal, and always verbal—sometimes shift or collapse. Our perceptions, it is true, are released within them, released or restrained. But our perceptions are realized also when the frames accidentally break or strain. Suddenly, what one frame excluded, another contains. And that thing itself becomes changed. I trust that these paracritical essays are moderately conscious of their contingencies as well as of their frames. Yet I would not wish them to be so self-reflexive as to vanish in a game of mirrors, or foolishly deny the mortality of every heart or art.

Enough said in this matter. Nietzsche offers this provocation: "As the man who acts must, according to Goethe, be without a conscience, he must also be without knowledge; he forgets everything in order to be able to *do* something. . . ." We, of course, can never forget; for reality forgives nothing. But we may induce that fortunate forgetfulness that permits an action to complete itself in an act of creation. The need to introduce these essays, then, may be spurious; it is certainly theoretically moot. I acknowledge in this preface the contradiction, and it will not be the last. But I acknowledge as well the right of every reader to ask: What is here?

At the center of my concerns is an awkward vision of change, a pressing query about the destiny of our race. What role will expanding human consciousness play in the universe? At the center, too, is an intuition that the imagination—the full in-forming power of mind, fictive legacy of all our dreams—may help to articulate, and indeed to shape, the convergent life of our race. Possibly this is a Romantic intuition. Or is it older than Plato's thought? No matter: its meaning must renew itself in particular encounters with our postmodern politics, technologies, arts. The term "postmodern" is itself much on my mind, and so appears frequently in this work. My definition of it remains highly tentative; for few can already see the moment whole. Silence may be an element of postmodernism, if by "silence" we intend a metaphor for many languages which place themselves in radical doubt. Such doubt challenges humanists to the limits of their patience, and that challenge is also one of my themes. Humanist culture is becoming a small part of our culture, and criticism a smaller culture still. Who, then, will be left to empower our metaphors, our dreams?

These are my concerns. Are they widely shared? The sixties are already behind us, and behind the reactions to their antinomian will. But what lies ahead? Jean Dubuffet says: "I have the impression that a complete liquidation of all the ways of thinking, whose sum constituted what has been called humanism and has been fundamental for our culture since the Renaissance, is now taking place, or, at least, going to take place very soon." This is not reassuring. How many can look beyond humanism, can carry forward a fundamental commitment to human Being into new and unthinkable forms? Let us admit it: there is a kind of terrorism abroad, even within the circles of art. We counter that terrorism with terror of our own—or counter it, more often, with emptiness, with nostalgia. I doubt that paracritical speculations can assuage the anxieties of the day.

Here I hope to be forgiven some personal notes. The days take care of themselves, and I find no pleasure in the literary fray. My own commitment is elsewhere; I am amateur of change. I have enjoyed my role as witness—often curious and sometimes confused—to the New. These have been within my purview: postwar American fiction; the literature of silence; the limitations of criticism, especially formalism; the dispositions of a postmodern society; technology; the future. On these subjects I have written early, and some would say written too early; I have taken certain risks of judgment.

Now risk, in the academic humanities, serves few functions; it cannot be highly esteemed. Ideas, persons, and events are accorded the status of a fad until they suddenly become part of history. In this climate of response, it is natural that my predilections should be sometimes regarded with suspicion. I confess that I do not often recognize myself in the image which suspicion reflects back upon me. But then, we all create images of one another, and many are variations on the same theme: self and other, saints and sinners, wise men and fools . . . the eternal dialectic. But why not a trialectic, for instance, or multilectic? In my own temperament, I know, at least three persons quarrel: an Existentialist, a Utopian, and an Orphist.

I spoke immodestly of risk; let me at least put the matter in perspective. There is freedom in intellectual risk, excitement, perhaps originality. But risk is not risk without its price: isolation, crankiness, the quick stab of doubt. I have paid, will continue to pay, the price. But one may learn from one's excesses, and others may learn even more. In any case, the chances I have taken in these speculations are not the largest a man could take. Nor have the penalties within my profession been intolerably harsh. To be denied a fellowship by the American Council of Learned Societies is more than a nuisance but hardly a crash.

The difficulties are not all personal. The terrorism of the age may leave a valuable residue: disconfirmation of familiar forms. Disconfirmation attends true creation; only that which offers itself to death can hope to receive new life. Yet what has disconfirmation in the humanities brought? Consider, for instance, Jacques Ehrmann's extreme view of literature: "Since its only viable status is as subversion, its function can only be a terrorizing one . . . of burning, consuming meaning. By this act, the reading-writing process makes manifest the impossibility of meaning." Or again, consider Tzvetan Todorov's view: "We must first cast a doubt upon the legitimacy of the very notion of literature; neither the mere existence of the term, nor the fact that a whole university system is based upon it, can of itself justify its acceptance." These statements appear in one of the finest theoretical quarterlies, misnamed *New Literary History* (not a history of the new!). Yet I doubt that many of its readers, I doubt that even its editors, are willing to carry the disconfirmation implied by such concepts to their practice of teaching or scholarship, still less, willing to renew their sense of the total human endeavor under the aspect of language.

Thus the humanities in general and criticism in particular, intent on the systemization of their most radical insights, end by exempting themselves from the hazards of innovation. Scholarship is ironic, as Nietzsche knew, and it is the ironic Nietzsche that the newest wave of scholarship—it is *not* a gay science—now rediscovers. But there are other waves that break on our mental shores. The various theories of Husserl, Heidegger, Wittgenstein, Lévi-Strauss, Saussure, the literary ideas of Michel Foucault, Jacques Derrida, Gilles Deleuze, Roland Barthes, after long neglect in American criticism, suddenly turn into a constant susurrus of abstract discourse that ignores its own insecurity and changes nothing. Nor are the masters always exempt from the charges against their epigones. Nor, of course, am I.

True, criticism now interrogates itself brilliantly, especially in France. And although I should like to stand at some readable distance from French criticism, there are a few questions that occur to me even now. A critic locks himself into a certain relation to an author, a text, a particular language or voice. Is all criticism, then, a rationalized response to a "voice" that the critic pretends to hear and which he never hears twice the same? As a "listener," the critic spends his time. Is critical time different from other kinds of human time? How? And what are the great failures of criticism? Are they failures of tact, method, or discrimination, as critics like to believe? Or are they antecedent failures of wisdom, the quality of the critic's life within literature and without? Again, what usable principle or perception may a critic derive from all the quarrels of criticism, the battles of books ancient and modern? Is there, in short, a phenomenology of critical conflicts? And how docile should criticism remain? To what extent is its duty, like that of "literature," to transgress? Then again, how can critical discourse adapt to new technologies and mixed media, new languages of the mediated and immediate mind? Need the critical and imaginative faculties remain always separate in expression? Or are there conditions under which their expressions may become one? Last, can criticism help to formulate a theory of change, and thus become part of a design of life? The questions abound; my last question is not really the last. There is at least one more I should like to ask: When will criticism confront the implications of its own queries, and what then will it become?

I have no answer. Yet I believe that an answer must go beyond our current shibboleths: disconfirmation, decreation, demystification, deconstruction, decentering, depropriation, difference, etc. Perhaps we need to go beyond Irony (as Nietzsche sometimes did), beyond the current aversion to Wholeness and Meaning, to some working faith in . . . what? The success of the universe? The faith of Sartre: "The real literary commitment, finally, is the fact of assuming the entire world— in its totality. To take the universe as a whole, with man inside"? For myself, I know I could not engage in the literary act without struggling for a sense of what it means to be human in the cosmos. Other critics may assign their large questions to a religion, ideology, or metaphysics, and thus free themselves to approach literature more discretely. Though such discreteness is not my way, I would not contest it so long as others do not suppose their tacit metaphysics to be also my own. In the end, I think, we err by refusing the largest questions, and err again by forgetting to raise these questions anew. But questions remain questions; they will never dissolve desire, dream, death. Like Sartre, another rough-hewn man, Solzhenitsyn, keeps his eyes on the living whole. In his Nobel lecture, he describes how he came to realize "that world literature was not an abstraction, not something which had not yet crystallized, something created by the scholars of literature, but was a certain common body and common spirit, a living unity of the heart, in which the growing spiritual unity of humanity was expressed. . . . there is no such thing left on our Earth as INTERNAL AFFAIRS."

The growing spiritual unity of humanity. I have never understood how anything less can do. The true environment of any form of life is always *all* of life, and that includes its horrors too. Somehow, the universe does not forgive a narrower loyalty. Meanwhile, we move through history. Meanwhile, we play out our politics. (We cannot do without politics; it will not do for us.) Meanwhile, we practice torture, which has become more prevalent than at any other time; and we turn the permanent revolution of hope into perpetual genocide. In short, we remain human: a cruel, crotchety, and self-creative race. This, too, is the business of criticism—humanist or posthumanist, as you will.

And what is human? The human brain is not whole; old instincts and new faculties clash; and when adrenalin shoots through the blood, reason gags. —Our psychic life remains tenebrous; the unconscious is the alien within; our motives speak in a babble of tongues. —Human survival required special effort from evolution; clawless, fangless, slow, we received a brain, a language, a wondrous aggressiveness. —We share the experience of life with all animals, and stand alone in the consciousness of death; self-awareness is awareness of mortality. Yet we desire immortality too, and thus wreak havoc on creation. —Infant and child depend on their parents longer than any other animal; this is how we acquire the skills and symbols of maturity. But dependence perpetuates the need for love. Who has not smashed another, asking for love? —Morality is the product of pain, conscience the product of guilt; thus we accuse ourselves to create society. —Culture derives from memory; but we also recall what we ought to forget. The memory of rage turns into spite and violence; to remember all is to forgive nothing. —We find freedom in fantasy; in fantasy everything is possible.

But fantasy becomes fact; the visions of Sade become the evidence of history. Without dreams, man could neither transcend himself nor violate his fellow man. —Human thought requires symbol, distance, abstraction; we remove ourselves from the flesh in order to manipulate the invisible. But the flesh remains; our navel is more real than any detonator for the doomsday bomb. —What, indeed, is human!

Perhaps in the end, in an end we still do not completely grasp, "human" is not enough. Intuitively most of us feel that we live for something that goes beyond our peculiar passions. What is its name? Perhaps we live for life. And life? Some, like Henri Bergson, might say: "Consciousness, or supraconsciousness, is the name for the rocket whose extinguished fragments fall back as matter. . . ." Others stand closer to the clay: for them life is simply change. Myself, I believe change is musical, and the music is not all of our making. How else give Time continuous value?

Milwaukee, Wisconsin   January, 1974

1

FRONTIERS OF CRITICISM
1963, 1969, 1972

PROLOGUE

The subject is frontiers, frontiers of criticism.

But men live perpetually in the shadow of their histories; what they call the present is already biography. Moreover, academies favor the party of memory, and wait for culture to reveal the shape of its energies. Moreover, literature seldom moves in the far front of culture; the other arts, released from the conservative hold of language, push ahead. Finally, criticism, weighed by its own skepticism, lags still behind the literature of its day. Truly, the frontiers of criticism stand somewhere between us and prehistory.

Need this always be so? The imagination empowers change, and every dreamer has his muse. Even critics must now and then improvise on the possible.

1963

Not long ago—or is it really ages past?—most students of literature, myself included, recognized the elegance of René Wellek's formulation of the destiny of criticism: "the interpretation of literature as distinct from other activities of man."[1] Coming from Professor Wellek, the emphasis on interpretation rather than on literary theory seemed unduly self-effacing. Be that as it may, the formula appealed then to the common rage for order, and seemed also to aver the dignity of the humanities on terms that the age demanded. With the years, however, the formula seems, to me at least, to have lost in elegance. The breed of technicians it has unwittingly sanctioned may have found a truer consummation of their hopes in the laboratories of Oak Ridge. Literature as a distinct activity of man? Criticism as a distinct response to a distinct activity of man? What is man that we should be so little mindful of him, so arbitrary with the complexities of his mind? From Surrealism to Absurdism, literature itself suggests that a distinct aesthetic response may be defined only at the risk of deadly discrimination.

Yet my object is not to engage in polemics. The point can be stated with some equanimity: a new breed of American critics are anxious to assert themselves against the rigors and pieties they have inherited. Their mood is restless, eclectic, speculative; sometimes it is even apocalyptic. Those who feel out of sympathy with them may wish to apply different epithets: romantic, primitivist, existential, amateurish, or plain anti-intellectual. (The usefulness of these tags, dispensed usually with contumely, is as doubtful as their accuracy.) Others, however, may recognize the creative possibilities of this new mood, troubled, vague, or disruptive as it may seem.

Evidence of the new mood is various, though one senses behind it the enduring search for wholeness and vitality in the literary response. One senses, too, the paradoxical desire to appropriate literature to the dream life of men and women, and then again to implicate it in the widest sphere of their daily actions. Is not the secret task, for poet and critic alike, to participate in that magic process whereby the word is turned into flesh?

The critic therefore feels the need for commitment; he wants to testify. And what is to prevent him? The encounter with an authentic work of art is a bruising experience, full of strange knowledge and hidden pleasure, of the kind we usually spend a lifetime resisting. The critic knows that he himself is on trial, and that the act of literary criticism is above all an act of self-judgment. Since his business is to speak of literature, speech in his case must ultimately take the form of self-revelation. But the need for self-revelation is not only a private or existential need. It is also a social function of the critic. "Is art always an outrage—must it by its very nature be an outrage?" Durrell asks.[2] The question haunts the critic even more than it does the censors of our time. For should the critic insist on his dubious right to privacy or detachment, his deepest knowledge of literature would remain locked, a private outrage, an inner wound. Yet literature, we know, acts through language; it is a communal call, there where words and experience are one, as it is solitary subversion, where words begin to fail. In the act of testimony, therefore, the critic admits the *relevance* of the buried power of literature; he offers himself to the harsh task of mediating between society and vision, culture and anarchy. There is the risk, of course, that such mediation may rob both culture and outrage of their particular force. Yet from that loss a new life in history may be gained, a new consciousness of self and society may be born. This is precisely the gain implicit in the discomforts of critical commitment which Lionel Trilling, in his otherwise subtle essay "On the Modern Element in Modern Literature," seems to ignore.[3]

Commitment, however, is but a single impulse of the new critical attitude; it simply prepares the ground for dialogue. Another impulse may be defined as the refusal to objectify the work of literature. The art work, of course, has been long considered as an object, an object for dissection or knowledge, idolatry or classification. Yet the encounter between critic and work is neither entirely objective nor purely aesthetic; it may be a "dialogue" of the kind Martin Buber has proposed. In Buber's sense, the work of art resists identification with the insensible It; for the work demands answer and response, and it requires a meeting. Is it then so perverse to ask the critic, whether he subscribes to Buber's theology or not, that he "turn toward" the work and confess with Buber, "in each instance a word demanding an answer has happened to me"?[4] Nothing is mystical in this statement, nothing inimical to the spirit of poetry. The statement, in fact, points to some rather mundane questions which Walter J. Ong, theologian of another faith, happily raises. In his original essay "The Jinnee in the Well-Wrought Urn," Father Ong states: "Creative activity is often . . . powered by the drive to accomplish, in terms of the production of an object of art, an adjustment in certain obscure relationships with other persons." What does this mean? The jinnee cannot be exorcised from the urn it inhabits, however shapely the latter may prove; the artifact still comes to life with voices unknown. And indeed this is what we, as readers, require. Once again Father Ong sees the point clearly: "As a matter of full, serious, protracted contemplation and love, it is unbearable for a man or woman to be faced with anything less than a person. . . ."[5] This is precisely what critics, compelled by the difficult reciprocities of love, may now want to face: not an object but a presence mediated cunningly, incomprehensibly, by language. Such a presence is not simply human. It is the presence, moving and participating in reality, which Owen Barfield, in *Saving the Appearances*, has shown us lies at the heart of the symbolic process. In facing such a presence, critics may hope to recover the primal connection with a universe mediated increasingly by abstractions. But they may also hope to recover something more modest: a spontaneity of judgment which reaches outward, reaches beyond itself.

If some postwar critics are loath to consider the literary work merely as an object, they are equally reluctant to believe that contemplation is the sole reaction to it. Beyond testimony, beyond participation or dialogue, the critic now wishes to entertain the possibility that *action* may be a legitimate response to art. By this, of course, I do not mean that he rushes to the barricades after reading *The Conquerors*, or that he develops tuberculosis after reading *The Magic Mountain*. I mean that the experience of a literary work does not leave him unchanged. To the extent that he is altered in the recesses of his imagination, indeed of his being, to that extent he must act differently in daily life. For if literature is both cognitive and experiential, as we have been so often told, then how can new knowledge but prompt new action? We may have accepted the Thomist notion of stasis in art much too uncritically. The counterstatement is boldly presented in Sartre's essay "Qu'est-ce que la littérature?" "Parler c'est agir," Sartre claims; "toute chose qu'on nomme n'est déjà plus tout à fait la même, elle a perdu son innocence." Sartre continues: "L'oeuvre d'art est valeur parce qu'elle est appel."[6] The appeal, above all, is to an act of self-definition and also of freedom. For in a sense, the work itself is "created" by the freedom of the reader to give it a concrete and, ultimately, personal meaning. The work, that is, finally enters the total existence of a man, not simply his dream life or aesthetic consciousness; and in doing so it becomes subject to the total judgment of human passions. This is precisely what an existential writer of a different breed, Camus, meant when he wrote, "To create today is to create dangerously. Any publication is an act, and that act exposes one to the passions of an age that forgives nothing. . . ."[7] But if the writer must create dangerously these days, the critic cannot afford to criticize timorously. Dangerous criticism assumes that final and somewhat frightening responsibility which some critics naturally resist; namely, the willing suspension of aesthetic judgment in the interests of right action.

I quite realize the enormity of this assertion. For one thing, it brings the critic dangerously close to the posture of the censor—the commissar, the propaganda helot, the prurient chief of police—who requires that every work of art display its social credentials or else stand convicted. No doubt the redemption of man is a more momentous task than the creation of beauty, and virtue and goodness confute their scoffers. Yet redemption, one suspects, does not lie in the grasp of regulators; nor does virtue depend on the degradation of art by power. How, then, can the critic hope to transcend the "aesthetic" domain of literature without seeming to capitulate to dogma or authority, without seeming to endorse a vulgar or repressive utilitarianism? Quite candidly, I have never found an answer wholly adequate to this query. In the end, we act as men or women, not as critics or scholars, and the demands of a particular moment compel us to reveal that value to which we choose to give precedence. That value engenders our momentary answer. Is there another that will hold for everyone, in every place and every time?

Critics have also begun to heed certain *thematic* questions which were once considered beneath notice. A number of works of the last decade reflect this emergent concern. In *The Tragic Vision*, for instance, Murray Krieger pertinently asks, "But how, if we limit ourselves to technical literary definitions, can we find for the tragic any meaning beyond that of Aristotle? The answer is, by moving from formalistic aesthetics to what I would term 'thematics.' " Krieger's analysis of that term cannot be summarized easily, but the implications of his method are stated succinctly enough. He concludes thus: "All of which is perhaps to say only that a literary theory must be adequate to the literary experiences for which it is to account and that we trust our way of experiencing literature only as it is adequate to the life out there, which cries for a way of being organized literarily that will yet leave it preserved intact."[8] If the insistence on "the life out there" does not necessarily force the critic into a study of "thematics," it does persuade him to dwell on precisely those formal matters that invoke the larger aspects of reality and may even engage religious thought. Thus the essays of James E. Miller, Jr., Karl Shapiro, and Bernice Slote, in *Start with the Sun*, explore the relation of Dionysian poetry to cosmic consciousness, mystery, and apocalypse. "Start with the sun:" Miss Slote ends, taking her cue from a noble phrase of Lawrence, "Perhaps then we may be absolved from the poetry of mirrors."[9] Parallel explorations of fiction lead R. W. B. Lewis to distinguish between the generation of Proust, Joyce, and Mann, in whose world the aesthetic experience was supreme, and the generation of Silone, Faulkner, Camus, and Greene, in whose world "the chief experience has been the discovery of what it means to be a human being and to be alive." Lewis continues: "Criticism, examining this world, is drawn to the more radically human considerations of life and death, and of the aspiring, sinful nature of man."[10]

Perhaps I have spoken long enough of certain interests of postwar criticism, though I feel I have spoken of them only tangentially. If one were to search for the theoretical basis of these interests—a task which I must leave to more philosophical critics—one might be inclined to develop a view of literature that does not put the idea of form at its center. By this I do not simply mean a redefinition of the concept of form so that it may account, say, for the plays of Beckett or the novels of Burroughs. I would plead for a more radical view. From Kant to Cassirer, from Coleridge to Croce and down to the New Critics, the idea of organic form has been a touchstone of value and a cornerstone of theory in literary study. We assume, and indeed we believe, that the imagination incarnates itself only as an aesthetic order, and that such an order is available to the analytic mind. We believe more: that aesthetic order defines the deepest pleasures of literature and conveys its enduring attractions. I am not at all secure in these beliefs. Indeed, I am willing to take the devil's part and entertain the notion that "structure" is not always present or explicable in literary works; and that where it reveals itself, it is not always worth the attention we give it. Such works as *Hamlet* and *Don Quixote* are not diminished by the discovery that their form, whatever it may be, is less organic than we expect the form of great works to be. Even that supreme artifact of our century, that total structure of symbols, puns, and cross-references, that city of words full of secret alleys and connecting catacombs, even Joyce's *Ulysses*, may prove to the keen, fresh eye of a critic more of a labyrinth, dead ends and ways without issue, than Dublin itself, which encloses the nightmare of history. This is precisely what Robert Martin Adams concludes in his fascinating study *Surface and Symbol*. Adams inspects minutely the wealth of details in the novel, and finds that many of them serve to blur or confuse rather than to sustain patterns: "The close reading of *Ulysses* thus reveals that the meaningless is deeply interwoven with the meaningful in the texture of the novel. . . . It is a book and an antibook, a work of art particularly receptive to accident. It builds to acute and poignant states of consciousness, yet its larger ambition seems to be to put aside consciousness as a painful burden."[11] Nothing catastrophic to the future of criticism is presaged by this statement. Quite the contrary: criticism may derive new vitality from some attention to the unstructured and even random element in literature. For is not form, after all, best conceived as a mode of awareness, a function of cognition, a question, that is, of epistemology rather than ontology? Its objective reality is qualified by the overpowering reality of human *need*. In the end, we perceive what we need to perceive, and our sense of pattern as of relation is conditioned by our deeper sense of relevance. This is why the aesthetic of the future will have to reckon with Freud, Nietzsche, and even Kierkegaard, who have given us, as well as Marx, compelling economies of human needs.

I could not persist in suggesting the theoretical implications of postwar criticism without falling into the trap which I have myself described. We do not always need a theoretical argument to bring forth a new critical attitude; we only need good critics. But perhaps we need, more than anything else, to regard literature in a more oblique fashion, regard it even in the slanting light of its own absurdity. We might then see that the theoretical solemnity of modern criticism ignores the self-destructive element of literature, its need for self-annulment. What Camus said of his own work applies, in various ways, to all literature: the act of creation is akin to chance and disorder, to which it comes through diversity, and it constantly meets with futility. "Creating or not creating changes nothing," Camus writes. "The absurd creator does not prize his work. He could repudiate it." And again: "The absurd work illustrates thought's renouncing of its prestige and its resignation to being no more than the intelligence that works up appearances and covers with images what has no reason. If the world were clear, art would not exist."[12] Perhaps the function of literature, after all, is not to clarify the world but to help create a world in which literature becomes superflous. And perhaps the function of criticism, as I shall argue later, is to attain to the difficult wisdom of perceiving how literature is finally, and *only* finally, inconsequential.[13]

The foregoing remarks limn certain trends in postwar criticism; they are not intended to define a school or movement. Still, I feel it wise to anticipate some objections before concluding this mock survey.

It may be argued, for instance, that many of the attitudes I have described are not so novel as I make them out to be. Richards' emotive theories, Burke's concept of action, Leavis' cultural vitalism, Trilling's depth-view of manners and imagination, Blackmur's metaphors of silence in literature, and above all, Herbert Read's sympathy for the anarchic spirit, certainly open the way to the speculations of younger critics. The latter, however, still distinguish themselves by a certain quality of passion, a generosity toward the perversities of spirit, and a sense of crisis in man's fate. In this respect, their sympathies flow toward Lawrence's seminal work, *Studies in Classic American Literature*.

Then again, it might be argued that my use of the terms "form" and "theory" appears tendentious; that, ideally speaking, neither of these terms excludes larger commitments; and that, in any case, there are so many concepts of "form" and "structure" in modern criticism as to make a general condemnation of them irresponsible. I would answer: what an ideal formalist theory may contribute to our appreciation of literature is not in dispute; what it has contributed in the past by way of practical criticism is also very considerable. Still, do we not all sense the growing inertness of the Spirit of criticism beneath the weight of the Letter? One sometimes feels that in another decade or two, the task of criticism may be safely performed by some lively computing machine which, blessed with total recall, would never misquote as some critics are reputed to do.

I speak, of course, hyperbolically. Perhaps I can make the point clearer, and sharpen thereby the distinction between two generations of critics, by referring to two eminent theoreticians of literature. Both René Wellek and Northrop Frye are men of vast erudition; both have shaped the course of literary studies in America. This, I think, is entirely as it should be; the timely authority of such works as Wellek and Warren's *Theory of Literature* or Frye's *Anatomy of Criticism* deserves nothing less. Yet at the risk of seeming ungracious, it is to their later, and perhaps lesser, works that I wish to refer. After all, the question still remains: what lies beyond formalist theory?

In *Concepts of Criticism*, Professor Wellek shows himself to be somewhat out of love with the directions of contemporary criticism. "It seems to me that in spite of the basic truth of the insight of organicism, the unity of content and form, we have arrived today at something like a deadend," he states.[14] His dissatisfaction, however, is of short duration. Professor Wellek sees the way out in the doctrine of "structuralism," evolved by the Prague Linguistic Circle—alas, now defunct! "Such a concept of the literary work of art avoids two pitfalls," Professor Wellek hopes: "the extreme of organicism which leads to a lumpish totality in which discrimination becomes possible, and the opposite danger of atomistic fragmentation."[15] The way out, as it turns out, comes very close to the ancient ideal of the golden mean. This is judicious. But is it really judiciousness which prompts him in two later chapters, "Philosophy and Postwar American Criticism" and "Main Trends of Twentieth-Century Criticism," to deride all recent criticism? The brilliant and inventive concern with American literature in the last two decades is deplored as an example of "romantic historicism," and mythic and existential criticism are condemned as an instance of "the irrationalistic philosophies of Europe" adapted to the pragmatic temper of the United States.[16] Professor Wellek sadly concludes: "Only those who adhere to either the German idealist tradition, in the Kantian or Coleridgean version, or those who rediscover Aristotle, still keep a grasp on the nature of art and recognize the necessity of an aesthetic and the ideal of a study of literature as literature."[17] Having defined literature in formalist terms, it is no wonder that Professor Wellek *still* believes formalist theory to be the most rewarding view of literature.

The Well-Tempered Critic, which is not wrought in the massive architectural manner of Professor Frye's earlier work, is too urbane to be tautological. Its urbanity expresses a fine subtlety of mind in the final chapter of the book, and the subtlety itself disguises a somewhat chilly view of literature. Professor Frye acknowledges the distinction between the classic and romantic tempers in criticism, and proceeds to discover the correlatives of each. The classic temper, he informs us, is aesthetic, the romantic is psychological; the former views art as artifact, the latter as expression; the one derives from Aristotle, the other from Longinus. I do not quarrel with these distinctions, particularly when categorical distinctions make the very basis of the geometric edifices Professor Frye likes to erect. "The first step to take here," he argues, "is to realize that just as a poem implies a distinction between the poet as man and the poet as verbal craftsman, so the response to a poem implies a corresponding distinction in the critic."[18] Again, Professor Frye views criticism not as the experience of literature but, more discretely, as an area of knowledge. This leads him to the hard-boiled conclusion, so repugnant to visionary educators, that "the values we want the student to acquire from us cannot be taught: only knowledge of literature can be taught."[19] Can knowledge be dissociated from value, and criticism forgo its aspiration to wisdom? Apparently so. "The fundamental act of criticism is a disinterested response to a work of literature in which all one's beliefs, engagements, commitments, prejudices, stampedings of pity and terror, are ordered to be quiet," he continues.[20]

Ordered to be quiet! Who listens, then, and who speaks instead? The imagination never demanded such frozen void, nor do the supreme fictions of the mind reject the earth they transmute. We have seen criticism gaze long enough on the world with the quiet eyes of Apollo. Shall we ever see it partake again of the sacred flesh of Dionysus? And why this mania for distinctions? Are there critics willing to speak professionally for the ancient female principle, acceptance and fusion, and the enveloping wholeness of things?

I do not wish to suggest that a Dionysiac vision is penetrating literary criticism the world over. I do sense, however, a movement in contemporary letters which must force us to revise our tenets or else accept the charge of theoretical isolationism in America. It is doubtful, for instance, that the plays of Beckett or Genet or Artaud, the novels of William Burroughs, Maurice Blanchot, or Alain Robbe-Grillet, the later stories of Salinger, the poetry of Charles Olson, René Char, Dylan Thomas—and I cite these names quite at random—can be illuminated brightly by the critical terms of Professors Wellek and Frye. Nathalie Sarraute's recent book, *The Golden Fruits,* and Marc Saporta's "shuffle novel," *Composition N° 1,* deny the conventional idea of structure. The first is a novel about a novel which cancels itself in the very act of reading; the second is a stratagem which accepts the principle of chance as an integral part of the literary experience. As for Burroughs' *The Soft Machine,* it applies—to what extent, no one will know—the "cut up method of Brion Gysin," a method which combines collage and montage. If these works possess a form, it is probably a "non-telic" form of the kind recently reflected in painting and music.[21] Must we then dismiss such works as faddish freaks, of more interest to literary gossip than literary history?

In France, where criticism has been long associated with the spirit of lucidity, critics take a different stand. A quick look at some of their statements may persuade us that their view of literature is not too far from the view I have proposed. The common theme of Claude Mauriac's *The New Literature* is stated thus: "After the silence of Rimbaud, the blank page of Mallarmé, the inarticulate cry of Artaud, a-literature finally dissolves in alliteration with Joyce. The author of *Finnegans Wake* in fact creates out of whole cloth words full of so many diverse overtones that they are eclipsed by them. For Beckett, on the contrary, words all say the same thing."[22] The theme of Roland Barthes' *Le Degré zéro de l'écriture* is similar: the avatar of the new literature is absence. Barthes writes: "Dans ces écritures neutres, appelées ici 'le degré zéro de l'écriture,' on peut facilement discerner le mouvement même d'une négation, comme si la Littérature, tendant depuis un siècle à transmuer sa surface dans une forme sans hérédité, ne trouvait plus de pureté que dans l'absence de tout signe, proposant en fin l'accomplissement de ce rêve orphéen: un écrivain sans Littérature."[23] Likewise, for Maurice Blanchot literature is moving toward "l'ère sans parole." This movement may lead to a form of writing that is incessant sound; or it may lead, as Blanchot states in *Le Livre à venir*, quite in the other direction: "La littérature va vers elle-même, vers son essence qui est la disparition."[24] Both directions, we can surmise, *end* in the dissolution of significant form, the abdication of language. Is this silence at the heart of modern literature the definition of outrage, a subjective correlative of our terror? Or is the monstrous language of action, which Bachelard believes to be pointing, beyond Lautréamontism, toward "une réintegration de l'humain dans la vie ardente . . . ," a closer correlative of that terror?[25] We can only observe that from Sade and Lautréamont to Kafka and Beckett the twin dark streams of poetry, the poetry of action and the poetry of silence, have been flowing toward some unknown sea wherein some figure of apocalypse, man or beast, still lies submerged.

Critics, however, are of many ilks, and for some the mantic role is as foreign as Elijah's. I wish to force no prophecies in the mouths of students of literature. Still, it is not unreasonable to ask that criticism evolve a method which takes deeper cognizance of the evolving character of life as of literature. The point is almost too obvious: contemporary letters can be judged as little by the standards of pure formalism as, let us say, Romantic poetry can be evaluated by the strict conventions of neo-Classicism.

The problem of criticism, however, must not be left to the indolent spirit of literary relativism. Indeed, the problem may not prove to be one of literary method at all. The problem of criticism is always the challenge of awareness, full awareness of human existence in time and in place, but also outside of both, in the dream world which antecedes all responsibilities. In the end, perhaps, the problem of critics and poets alike is one of human destiny. To say less is to confuse cowardice with modesty.

If there is an underlying theme in recent American criticism, it is the implicit theme of crisis, a crisis not merely of literary method but of literature itself, which means of culture and consciousness. The crisis, as Nicolas Berdyaev knew, is not the crisis of humanism but of humanity itself. In the past, periods of crisis have often bred visions of apocalypse.[26] Such visions may come our way again. They may even lurk in a critic's perplexity. Here is how Krieger put the question: "Or is it, perhaps, that the Kierkegaardian version is right and that our world has itself become the tragic visionary in its unbelief using self-destructive crises to force itself finally to confront the absurdities of earthly reality . . . ? Which is to ask, fearfully and even unwillingly, whether we have not been beguiled by aesthetic satisfactions and whether the utterly stripped tragic vision may not after all be less illusory than the fullness which shines through tragedy."[27]

This is no time to sit in judgment on the world or to interpret its modern tragedy. From the Revelation of St. John the Divine to Norman O. Brown's extraordinary Phi Beta Kappa address, entitled "Apocalypse," men have envisioned the destruction of the world and foreseen its resurrection. "Blessed and holy is he that hath part in the first resurrection: on such the second death hath no power . . . ," St. John says.[28] But we are not at the first resurrection yet; we are not even beyond madness. Thus from Norman O. Brown: "The alternative to mind is certainly madness. . . . Our real choice is between holy and unholy madness: open your eyes and look around you—madness is in the saddle anyhow."[29] What task will criticism perform, wavering between holy and unholy madness? What bootless task?

Criticism is no country for old men of any age. Criticism, which was born to behold literature, must still do so and look beyond itself. Tact and rigor may attend all our words, but our words will avail nothing if man prevails not. What lies beyond criticism? D. H. Lawrence put it thus in his *Apocalypse*: "O lovely green dragon of the new day, the undawned day, *come, come* in touch, and release us from the horrid grip of the evil-smelling old Logos! Come in silence, and say nothing. Come in touch, in soft new touch like a spring-time, and say nothing."[30]

NOTES

1 René Wellek, *Concepts of Criticism*, ed. Stephen G. Nichols, Jr. (New Haven, 1963), p. 343.

2 Lawrence Durrell and Alfred Perles, *Art and Outrage: A Correspondence about Henry Miller* (New York, 1961), p. 9.

3 Lionel Trilling, "On the Modern Element in Modern Literature," *Partisan Review Anthology*, ed. William Phillips and Philip Rahv (New York, 1962), pp. 267ff.

4 Martin Buber, *Between Man and Man* (Boston, 1955), p. 10.

5 Walter J. Ong, S.J., *The Barbarian Within* (New York, 1962), pp. 19, 25.

6 Jean-Paul Sartre, *Situations II* (Paris, 1948), pp. 72, 98.

7 Albert Camus, *Resistance, Rebellion, and Death* (New York, 1961), p. 251.

8 Murray Krieger, *The Tragic Vision* (New York, 1960), pp. 2, 244.

9 James E. Miller, Jr., Karl Shapiro, and Bernice Slote, *Start with the Sun* (Lincoln, Neb., 1960), p. 238.

10 R. W. B. Lewis, *The Picaresque Saint* (Philadelphia and New York, 1959), p. 9.

11 Robert Martin Adams, *Surface and Symbol: The Consistency of James Joyce's Ulysses* (New York, 1962), pp. 245, 253.

12 Albert Camus, *The Myth of Sisyphus* (New York, 1959), pp. 72ff.

13 These heretical statements are developed more fully in my essay "The Dismemberment of Orpheus," *American Scholar*, XXXII (Summer, 1963), pp. 463–484.

14 Wellek, p. 65.

15 *Ibid.*, p. 68.

16 *Ibid.*, pp. 333ff.

17 *Ibid.*, p. 342.

18 Northrop Frye, *The Well-Tempered Critic* (Bloomington, Ind., 1963), p. 123.

19 *Ibid.*, p. 136.

20 *Ibid.*, p. 140.

21 See Leonard B. Meyer, "The End of the Renaissance," *Hudson Review*, XVI (Summer, 1963), pp. 169–186.

22 Claude Mauriac, *The New Literature* (New York, 1959), p. 12.

23 Roland Barthes, *Le Degré zéro de l'écriture* (Paris, 1959), p. 12.

24 Maurice Blanchot, *Le Livre à venir* (Paris, 1959), p. 237.

25 Gaston Bachelard, *Lautréamont* (Paris, 1963), p. 154.

26 H. H. Rowley, *The Relevance of Apocalyptic*, rev. ed. (New York, n.d.), pp. 150–178.

27 Krieger, p. 21.

28 Revelation 20:6.

29 Norman O. Brown, "Apocalypse," *Harper's*, May, 1961, p. 47.

30 D. H. Lawrence, *Apocalypse* (Florence, 1931), pp. 233ff.

1969

1

Criticism engages new sounds of silence; metaphors of a new perception of literature are all around us.

Quick Queries

Who elucidates the contemporary imagination?

Is it the critics? Or is it the new troubadours, Leonard Cohen, Bob Dylan, Jacques Brel, John Lennon?

Criticism is still hermeneutic. But when will hermeneutics heal a culture, through clarification help to make it whole?

Queries End

McLuhan heralds the end of print; the "Gutenberg galaxy" is in process of burning itself out. Electric technology can dispense with words, and language may be "shunted" on the way to universal consciousness. Norman O. Brown predicts that "the rest is silence." The fall into language must be redeemed; "the infant of ineffable word" will lead us back to silence, "the mother tongue." And George Steiner speaks of a "Pythagorean genre," a radical experimental tradition in Western literature, which carries "inside it a potential of silence, the recognized possibility that literature may be insufficient."

For nearly a century, an extreme vision has pressed on language, forcing it to the edge of consciousness; the tension between Word and Flesh, now and there, begins to snap. Criticism must learn to acknowledge this force. Criticism must even learn to define its aims with metaphoric consent to its end. For there is a peculiar wisdom that we attain only when we consent to old ends and new beginnings.

2

I pass to another metaphor. The Logos may not yet disappear into mute matter or pure consciousness, but language will soon respond to new sciences and new technologies. Two decades ago, Norbert Wiener argued that languages are not "independent, quasi-biological entities, with their developments modified entirely by internal forces and needs." "In fact," Wiener said, "they are epiphenomena of human intercourse, subject to all the social forces due to changes in the pattern of that intercourse." In cybernetics, the organism is considered a pattern of messages, and messages can be coded and decoded in innumerable ways. Thus, the role of the word in mediating, in creating, the needs of culture may be radically modified.

But cybernetics is not the only science relevant to language. Biochemistry and neurophysiology promise to alter entirely our idea of man. Cloning, parthenogenesis, transplantation, prosthesis, the control of memory, intelligence, and behavior, the definition of genetic traits, of sex and life span, the creation of chimeras and androids, these, as Gordon Rattray Taylor says, are either here or soon to be in our midst:

> Professor Jean Rostand has dramatized the biological novelty of this new man by describing its characteristics: a strange biped that will combine the properties of self-reproduction without males like the greenfly; of fertilizing his female at long distances like the nautiloid mollusc; of changing sex like the xiphophores; of growing from cuttings like the earthworm; of replacing its missing parts like the newt; of developing outside its mother's body like the kangaroo and of hibernating like the hedgehog.

The result, I am sure, will prove more photogenic than Professor Rostand implies, and I hope more benevolent. But the point remains: humanism as we have known it, intermittently, for three thousand years, may no longer hold, may no longer suffice. Literature, perhaps more than any other art, has sustained the image of man; literature has been the carrier of humanism. And criticism, more than literature itself, has been jealous of the letter even more than the spirit of humanism.

How will criticism speak when humanism ceases to breathe? How will criticism survive?

3

A

Many the wonders but nothing walks stranger than man.
This thing crosses the sea in the winter's storm,
making his path through the roaring waves.

. . . .

Gay nations of birds he snares and leads,
wild beast tribes and the salty brood of the sea,
with the twisted mesh of his nets, this clever man.
He controls with craft the beasts of the open air,

walker on hills. The horse with his shaggy mane
he holds and harnesses, yoked about the neck,
and the strong bull of the mountain.

Language, and thought like the wind
and the feelings that make the town,
he has taught himself, and shelter against the cold,
refuge from the rain. He can always help himself.

B

What a piece of work is man! how noble in reason!
how infinite in faculty! in form and moving how express
and admirable! in action how like an angel! in apprehension
how like a god! the beauty of the world! the paragon of animals!
And yet, to me, what is this quintessence of dust?

4

The threats to humanism are not only technological.

Certainly, we have already felt intimations of man's sudden end as man in the landscapes of total terror. There is a silence on the other side of outrage that literature already knows: see Elie Wiesel's *Night*. The critical record is in Frederick Hoffman's *The Mortal No*, is in George Steiner's *Language and Silence*. "Has our civilization, by virtue of the inhumanity it has carried out and condoned . . . forfeited its claim to that indispensable luxury which we call literature?" Steiner asks. How will literature live on the lips of the inhuman? What will criticism say? Perhaps criticism can only cry: never, never, never. . . .

Yet humankind and its arts have well endured. The flash of fore-knowledge was in that chiseling eye at Altamira or Lascaux. True: we remain quiddities in the cosmos, made aliens by our consciousness. We create the Self and the Other so that they may lock in bloody embrace. For some, this is proof of existence. For others, the proof is in self-creation.

A Digression on Museums

There are many things to see in Scandinavia, which I visited one summer. There is Finland, for instance, a total AnviRonmenT where art and nature fuse in candle and lake, vase and tree, green eyes and slate of sky. There are also museums: national museums, city museums (full of civic bric-a-brac), galleries of modern art, special exhibits. Among the latter I recommend:

a.   The Mannerheim Museum in Helsinki

b.   The Hvitträsk Museum of Saarinen, near Helsinki

c.   The Wasa Museum, in Stockholm

d.   The Viking ships at Bygdøy, in Oslo

e.   The Royal Armory in Copenhagen (one face of old Denmark, and the other is Tivoli)

But I must return to my topic.

There is an eerie contrast between the new museums of art, airy and bright

(the Milles Garden in Stockholm, Vigeland Park and the Munchmuseet in Oslo, Louisiana outside Copenhagen)

and the great national museums, gloomy structures heavy with Stone Age sleep

(only in Stockholm is it functional and light).

The national museums begin at the beginning, end before our time.

They start with shards, arrowheads, burial mounds (the place of death is also where life curls around).

Soon we see Nordic ornaments; the Vikings arrive with their obelisque swords and golden greed, their ships

(shallow and straked like the baleen whale, these long boats with high dragon prows slice oceans of wind)

on to Christianity, its naked saints, its knights in iron

(slow, slow, culture emerges from ice and the winter dark; the sword cuts and thrusts, the pot feeds; men wander and women weave; with infinite cunning or ferocity, something presages Ibsen and Strindberg, Milles and Munch, Saarinen and Sibelius)

finally, the white dream of the Scandinavian welfare state.

Moving through these great houses of time, I moved in a musty trance. Yet I felt there as close to the central endeavor we call human as one does in a dance hall or deserted battlefield. Even museums sing:

> La Nature est un temple où de vivants piliers
> Laissent parfois sortir de confuses paroles;
> L'homme y passe à travers des fôrets de symboles
> Qui l'observent avec des regards familiers.

Can nature speak through whorls of a Viking brooch? Or through a sword, edge hacked, sculpted slowly by brine and earth? This nature that speaks may be a kinder consciousness and presages no end to man. Unless the inhuman disposes.

5

But postmodern literature knows silences other than the inhuman imposes. The avant-garde finds ingenious ways to deny language, deny form, deny art. These ways often generate new kinds of art. Let me briefly summarize five metaphors of anti-art:

A. Art cancels itself. The Tinguely machine works to destroy itself. The blank page and the white canvas pretend to deny their existence. The last sentence of Beckett's *How It Is* tells us that the book is about "how it wasn't." This radical irony is implicit in the statement of the Cretan who pretends that all Cretans are liars.

B. Art deprecates itself. "The idea of beauty has infected us all with sickness," the Dadaists said, and their latter-day followers cheer. Art also pretends to be absurd. "Creating or not creating changes nothing," Camus said. "The absurd creator does not prize his work. He could repudiate it." Neither art nor reason can elucidate existence.

C. Art becomes a self-reflexive game. In the foolish courts of civilization the Fool is King. The spirit of play dominates Camp, pornography, happenings. The spirit of numbers dominates the cool world of binary aesthetics. The game becomes a game of modular combinations, algebraic permutations, self-regarding fictions. The forms call attention to their miraculous or ludicrous emptiness.

D. Art orders itself loosely, even at random. Organic form becomes discontinuous, decentered, or aleatory form. The author does not impose his pattern on the material; it is no longer a question of bringing order out of chaos. The author invites participation; he increases the options of men. Thus the barrier between author and reader, creator and consumer, melts away. Both become discoverers of worlds that neither controls for the other.

E. Art refuses interpretation. Fancy pretends to be fact. And vice versa. Not an image of the soup can, but the soup can itself, the found object autographed. The novel as history; the nonfiction novel. The feigned concreteness of art mutes the shieking self. It also confesses itself helpless before the outrages of the day. No Gothic fiction is stranger than our newscasts.

But the definitive statement on anti-art is made by John Cage, standing in the shade of Marcel Duchamp:

> nothing is accomplished by writing a piece of music
> nothing is accomplished by hearing a piece of music
> nothing is accomplished by playing a piece of music
> our ears are now in excellent condition

As a statement, this reveals a sacramental disposition that Cage shares with few artists. The excellence of our senses, the redemption of our consciousness, the perfection of the human community, tend to make art superfluous. But the motives lurking in neo-Dadaism, pop art, process art, funk art, computer art, concept art, process art, *choseisme*, *tel quelisme*, etc., are more mixed. They range from the sacramental to the nihilistic. More often, the attacks on arts and letters are neither holy nor demonic; they are simply coy, joyous, or angry invocations of new dispositions of the imagination.

Of this we can be certain. Criticism goes slowly where literature goes. And the literature of the moment counterfeits its end. As if the tail could swallow the serpent's head!

Exhortation

Please read, on a sunny or rainy day, sitting in a rattan chair or eating a pomegranate, one, two, three, or none of the following works:

1. Philippe Sollers' *Nombres*
2. John Barth's *Lost in the Fun House*
3. Any copy of *Aspen*, especially No. 5 + 6, in which Susan Sontag's "The Aesthetics of Silence" appears.

6

Aspen raises an old issue anew. The issue is mixed media, intermedia, back to Wagner and to the French Symbolists, forward to the performances of Black Mountain College in 1952, and of Ann Halperin in 1969.

The issue is old; this does not mean that criticism has resolved it. Imagine the Magic Theatre at the Nelson Atkins Gallery in Kansas City—shades of Kafka's Natural Theatre of Oklahoma? Here is the ad for the Magic Theatre:

How about a trip that will dissolve the floors of memory and identity, becloud the boundaries separating reality and illusion, return the traveler momentarily to his primal, psychic self—all without benefit of hallucinogens?

Imagine, say, a poetry reading in that context. Farfetched? No. At the new Electric Circus in New York, Salvatore Maritarano produced "L's G. A.," a poetry reading based on Lincoln's Gettysburg

Address, projected through an amplified gas mask, to the accompaniment of tape, strobe, and film. What do we, literary critics, know that can guide our response, direct our bemusement, fashion our judgment of the case? The case is not unique. I have on my desk a novel—let us call it that—by a gifted young man—let us say gifted. It is a collection of dramatic sketches, jocular poems, aphorisms, drawings, and cutouts. It has been on my desk for some time, but my critical theory remains silent.

7

John Cage recounts two anecdotes in *A Year from Monday:*

A

A mother and son visited the Seattle Art Museum. Several rooms were devoted to the work of Morris Graves. When they came to one in which all of the paintings were black, the mother, placing a hand across her son's eyes, said, "Come, dear, mother doesn't want you to see these things."

B

More than fifty years ago, Marcel Duchamp "called attention to the value of things to which value was not ordinarily attached." On one occasion, a CBC interviewer asked him what he was doing now. Duchamp replied: "I breathe."

8

We are moving ever closer to the traditional concerns of the critic; we are moving—stepping-stones in a garden?—toward more familiar quandaries. The critic now rebels against narrow definitions of the literary response; he rebels against distinctions. His ideal is to exclude nothing from his attention. Is he mistaken?

Example

Jerzy Kosinski is an author. He has written two extraordinary novels, *The Painted Bird* and *Steps*. Certain responses to these works, particularly to the first, remind us that the force of literature can sweep before it our discernments.

Two burly Poles appeared one day at Kosinski's doorstep. They had read *The Painted Bird,* considered it a slur on the Polish nation, and bad for the import of Polish ham. They wanted to punish Kosinski, and destroy the printing press that his apartment, so they thought, contained. The author practiced on them some deceptions, very similar to the deceptions his artwork contained.

On another occasion, a young man sat down on the same doorstep, drinking beer and singing into the night. He could not be removed. He too had read *The Painted Bird,* considered it a work of very personal significance. The youth proved to be the editor of a college paper. He was sent to Vietnam, and wrote several times a month to Kosinski. These letters, I understand, are minor masterpieces on the arts of death.

Example Ends

Author and reader now meet everywhere: in language, on the stair, on the telescreen. The old distinctions between art and life are distinctions that few contemporary artists find interesting to maintain. The academic definition of literature is, like most definitions, only part of a much larger whole. So too: the discourse of the critic, in class or quarterly, is partial; his words touch the fringes of literature. That is why the critic must learn that nothing finally needs to be said about literature.

And what exactly lies beyond criticism? The erotics of participation? The perpetual effort of self-creation?

9

Let us continue: if we need a literary theory at all, it is a theory of playful discontinuity. The most vigorous thought of our day has given itself to experience the creative possibilities within continuous forms, between these forms, without these forms. This is perhaps the main point that Frank Kermode misses in his penetrating study, *The Sense of an Ending.*

The sense of discontinuity is hard for critics to achieve. They have been raised on the doctrine of organic form. Here, for instance, is Northrop Frye: "The primary understanding of any work of literature has to be based on an assumption of its unity. However mistaken such an assumption may eventually prove to be, nothing can be done unless we start with it as a heuristic principle."

This is an important, a vastly influential, statement. Unfortunately, contemporary arts do not gladly corroborate it. A novel by Burroughs, a poem by Queneau, a painting by Johns, a film by Warhol, a sculpture of Oldenburg, a piece of music by Stockhausen may share another principle. The principle, as in Dada, is perhaps one of playful discontinuity. The principle is not frivolous. Even language begins to break as culture moves toward new centers of energy. We are not surprised to read of Marcuse's darker interest in the matter: "The word refuses the unifying, sensible rule of the sentence. It explodes the preestablished structure of meaning and, becoming an 'absolute object' itself, designates an intolerable, self-defeating universe—a discontinuum." Yet we still prefer to put the text before us, and to exhaust ourselves in perceiving the intricacies of its parts. We become irate when Norman O. Brown says: "The basic assumption of modern hermeneutics, the organic unity of the document, is a commitment to univocation; and was elaborated by Protestantism to set up the one true meaning of scripture."

Criticism should learn about playful discontinuity and become itself less than the sum of its parts. It should offer the reader empty spaces, silences, in which he can meet himself in the presence of literature. This is paracriticism: an attempt to recover the art of multivocation. Not the text and its letters but metaphors thereof. Not a form strictly imposed but the tentativeness between one form and another. In old dreams—the testament of our broken lives—begin our new responsibilities. Shatter the mirrors.

10

A dream. The journey began heroically though the landscape was cluttered. The landscape offered many dangers, of time and bulk and color. He conquered without effort, without benefit of knowledge. Behind his eyes all was lucid. But the landscape narrowed, and ciliate forms closed upon him from every side. He drove ahead, clearing the path of his will. And still the landscape narrowed. Smooth walls of a cavern, veined and wet. Fear pulled at his breath. The funnel, smoother now than onyx, narrowed. For the first time he turned around, seeking a memory of space, of light. Behind him the clarity of a mirror walled his sight. He plunged again, driven now by a greater fright, and as he moved into a thin channel scarcely larger than his head, the mirror closed behind, sealing all regress.

When he awoke, he believed all the mirrors had melted into a stream, and the sea felt fuller.

11

We can now move closer to the scene of contemporary criticism. The metaphors of an altered perception of the critical mind are scattered in it, blank spaces in a mosaic of statements, of attitudes, of recognitions. The mosaic is not fixed in a single pattern. Every year, every decade, the pieces fall, and the pattern is made over again. The pattern itself can be seen in various ways.

I offer this random mosaic of criticism.

a.   The Dutchman, Menno Ter Braak, says: "We do not proclaim ourselves for or against poetry here, we only take sides against the deification of the form . . . at the expense of the creative being; we defend the notion that the personality is the first and last criterion in judging an artist."

b.   The Frenchman, Roland Barthes, says: "The very definition of the work changes: it is no longer an historical fact; it becomes an anthropological fact, since no history exhausts it. The variety of senses does not depend on a relativistic view of human customs; it designates, not an inclination of society to error, but a disposition of the work to openness. . . ."

c.   Another Frenchman, Maurice Blanchot, says: "Literature is that experience through which consciousness discovers its being in its inability to lose consciousness . . . it reconstitutes for itself, beyond unconsciousness, a haggard knowledge, which knows nothing, which no one knows, and which ignorance finds always behind itself, like its shadow changed into a look."

d.   The Swiss, Jean Starobinski, says: "In recompense, I will feel a glance arising from the work and directed on me: this glance is not the reflection of my interrogation. It is a foreign consciousness, radically other . . . the work interrogates me."

e.   The German, Walter Benjamin, says: "With the increasing extension of the press . . . an increasing number of readers became writers. . . . It began with the daily press opening to its readers space for 'letters to the editor.' . . . Thus, the distinction between author and public is about to lose its basic character. The difference becomes merely functional; it may vary from case to case. At any moment, the reader is ready to turn into a writer. . . . Literary license is now founded on polytechnic rather than specialized training and thus becomes common property."

f.   The Belgian, Georges Poulet, says: "A literary text is above all a living, conscious reality, a thought that thinks to itself and which, in thinking, becomes thinkable to us—a voice that speaks to itself and which, in so speaking, speaks to us from within."

g.   The American, Morse Peckham, says: "I have attempted to show that the notion that all works of art and all aesthetic experiences have something in common is in error, that art is a disjunctive category, established by convention, and that art is not a category of perceptual fields, but of role-playing."

h.   And the great Canadian, Northrop Frye, whose heart is really not in this matter, nevertheless says: "Our society appears to be in a revolutionary phase in which the revolutionary side of the movement has been more successful than the Marxist movement of thirty years ago was in capturing the loyalties of creative and articulate people. The revolution of our time . . . is rather a psychologically based revolution, a movement of protest directed at the anxieties of privilege. . . . A revolutionary movement of this kind is one in which the arts can play a central and functional role. . . . Some issues which a generation ago were largely literary conventions have now become expanded and clarified as social issues."

But what of it?

I do *not* say that these prophets always confirm my sense of the frontiers of criticism

I do *not* say that they agree with one another, and form a cult or school

I do *not* say that they epitomize their critical theory in the statements I have quoted

And I do *not* say that they exhaust the range of critical opinions in the modern world.

I do say that in this mosaic of statements a certain pattern or movement may be discerned. It is a movement away from the literalism of criticism, away from its previous formal and historical definitions. It is a movement that explores the subjective life, the silent structure of language and of consciousness, and implicates criticism into a wider experience, the fantasy of culture. It is a movement, beyond the control of the art object, toward the openness, and even the gratuitousness—gratuitous is free—of existence. Perhaps it is even a movement toward the generalization of our attention in an age that heralds universal leisure, the end of specialization—a movement, therefore, that seeks to adapt the literary response to new conditions of survival.

12

The handwriting on the wall is always invisible. It becomes legible only when the wall begins to crumble. But this is easy to claim. My metaphors of a new critical perception may be intellectual fictions of my own. The case must now come to rest in our sense of rigor and hope. The issue is larger than criticism. There is a power in literature that enhances our presence as it recovers the infinitude of human consciousness. That same power, richly felt, adapts the future to our needs. That same power fits our will to evolution.

Let criticism, then, become a design for life. Let it envision a new man. Let it also praise, and thus foster mutability. This I know: at the frontiers, things come together. The frontiers are "pressant."

1972

The literary process is both publicity and concealment. It baffles everyone, eludes the vain, the innocent, the cynical. Art and politics, sex and money, history and neurosis, mind and malice—and a hundred intangible realities of the moment—enter into it. Yet many continue to perform the literary act like bright seals in search of the last silvery herring.

I, too, have my habits and ritual performances. I write a book in longhand. I revise it with eraser and pencil. My wife types it, and I proofread the typescript with a pen. My copyeditor, at the publishing house, goes over the manuscript with a color pencil, and returns certain pages with queries. I then wait for the galleys, which I correct. Later the page proofs arrive, and I correct these too. I then receive unbound copies of the book; they go to advance readers and a few friends. Finally, a year later, or perhaps two: "the finished product." Are these the uses of real, of lived time? My habits serve a dead man.

Yet this is only the start. The book is out, and its author pretends, in reviews and interviews, to be still alive. Let us say the book is titled *The Dismemberment of Orpheus: Toward a Postmodern Literature* (New York: Oxford University Press, 1971). Obscure things begin to happen. For instance: "ReMembrance of Orpheus, in Seven Voices, One Silent."

(Can you name the seven?)

I

The Literary Cynic:

There's something strange in this literary business, something satisfying but also vicious. Satisfying because vicious? Forget causality; the business is just strange. Now, I don't mean that telepathy and telekinesis are already making print obsolete—someday they may— nor yet the hologram. I mean curious. Ask Larry Sterne. Ask the Romantics or the Surrealists. This old uneasiness with literature, writing books, publishing them, reading them, offering endless critiques. . . .

"I too dislike it."

Literature squabbling and wrangling with itself forever, only to

make itself new. Very cute. Or should I say sickly? And now the
wrangling has come to autoreviews! But why should he, who pretends
to be so well at ease within his own skin, write at all?

II

The Reviewer:

I have always believed, and probably always shall, that the proper
way to begin a book review is with the Table of Contents. Here it is:

III

The Professor:

They say Knowledge is Power. Writing a book is an act of aggression. But
also one of self-exposure. Writing a book, then, one enters the endless cycle of
Victimizer and Victim. This cycle must be broken.

The avoidance of Power presents a special problem to writers of antinomian temper. They fail because the alternative to Power is still undiscovered.
The alternative (it is not Love) seems closer to the Void.

This came to me as I worked my way slowly through historical Europe,
journeying ever northward. Everywhere, the king and bishop, the general and
judge, statues in circles or great squares, thrones and tapestries, arms on display, entrances and exits through myriad eyes—everywhere, in short, manifesta-

tions of Power in relation to Others! It suddenly occurred to me: without the Other, no Power. The price, then, is Solipsism?

Let me offer an instance. The author of a recent book, *The Dismemberment of Orpheus,* seems to share with the writers he treats a certain radical view of existence. They seek a new language of Consciousness. They, too, want to escape the Other in their alien poetry. Judge their success by the fate of the Marquis de Sade: power-crazed, he became a master solipsist in the dungeon of his dreams, then escaped into literature by the back door, now a Public Figure.

This is inevitable in the Age of Media. For a mass medium "creates" a work of art, an event, or a statement, just as much as its author. Perhaps more! The Medium is the Noise of the Other preempting the Self. The latter can only control the former by becoming itself Another—witness the example of Mailer, his myths and masks. Witold Gombrowicz once said: "Not only do I give myself meaning. Others also give me meaning. Out of this collision of interpretations arises a third interpretation which characterizes me."

IV

The Reviewer:

Let me say at once that *The Dismemberment of Orpheus* (1971) is a kind of literary history, not of Modernism but of Postmodernism; it is anticipated history. It selects from the past a tradition which moves "toward a literature still to come." Hassan does not wish to deprecate the masters of Modernism: Proust, Joyce, Yeats, Valéry, Eliot, Kafka, Faulkner, etc. He only suggests that, questions of individual greatness aside, some align themselves with Postmodern directions —Kafka, for instance, and the early Hemingway—and that certain movements relegated by Edmund Wilson to an appendix—for example, Dada and Surrealism—are now central to our culture. To say it in pictures: young artists now eye Picasso less than Marcel Duchamp.

Yet it seems curious that Hassan should omit from his discussion Gertrude Stein and the Joyce of *Finnegans Wake.* Surely, both acted as nodes, points of contact between Modern and Postmodern literature. Both evolved a language that new writers have hardly begun to explore or exploit. The omission points to Hassan's weakness for symmetry; this "connoisseur of chaos" must keep his book in balance. Thus the four authors he chooses to discuss at length—masters of omission, of indeterminacy, of negativity, of silence—also represent American, German, French, and Irish literature, *one* of each. This book is rigid—and elusive as well.

V

The Literary Cynic:

Tell me, friend, just how does a book make its way? Is it rumor or review? Well, both are really the same. They say, for instance, that The New York Times Book Review, *which is getting better and better, will only review books by its own reviewers. That should fix him; they've ignored his last three books quite. The literary life, like most human endeavors, "short, nasty, and brutish." Velleities and articulations. The malice of the mind: in these very sentences. Cripples and grotesques, Napoleons of the pencil stub, chic undergroundlings, thrive equally in the republic of words. Then there are those blurbs that publishers extract from the author who in turn extorts them from his friends. Most undignified, I would say, and so rarely useful. And if used, all the qualifiers elided. Here are some of his friends. Alphabetically please!*

> *Ever since I read his first book I have considered Ihab Hassan one of the most original and stimulating critics of modern literature now writing in America. His new book shows the searching and provocative liveliness that one expects of Hassan's work. I don't always agree with what he says, and there are a few passages that I am not sure I understand, but the main point is that it is intellectually challenging and exciting.*
>
> David Daiches

> *Hassan combines a characteristically Existentialist awareness with the kind of fascination with the structure of consciousness associated with the current French tendency, and this in turn with an almost prophetic affirmativeness. This makes him one of the few current American critics who are a pleasure to read. And the pleasure of disagreeing with him is tremendous.*
>
> W. M. Frohock

> *Ihab Hassan moves with ease among the crags and pitfalls of avant-garde literature. From this terrain he is able to spy the moon lakes of postmodernism.* The Dismemberment of Orpheus *confronts the Silence and Fright that*

are conditions of the contemporary imagina-
tion.

Harold Rosenberg

In The Dismemberment of Orpheus, *Ihab*
Hassan has given us the definitive account of
the new avant-garde, in all of its aggressively
post-modern contemporaneity. It is, unques-
tionably, one of the most brilliant and
genuinely illuminating assessments of literary
life today that we now have.

Nathan A. Scott, Jr.

I have just finished The Dismemberment of
Orpheus. *I began it as a study of advanced*
modernist themes in which I am greatly inter-
ested. But I finished it as a serious, original
and passionate piece of work in its own right.
In pushing to the outer limits of conceptuali-
zation, as Hassan does, he engages, as almost
no other critic I know of, the material of the
writers in question on their own ground.

Daniel Stern

Depositions under subtle duress! But you should see some of the
other reviews. Or perhaps I should say hear. One or two emitted
noises that may remind you of some simian creature, gibbering its last
protest against extinction, or perhaps some courtly hyena gnawing
quietly at its entrails. Now, now, this isn't very nice. Writers and
reviewers, editors and scholars, it seems they're all made of the same
emory cloth. In the end, it all comes back to what Sartre replied to
Camus: "Whom did you expect to convince except my enemies and
your friends?"

VI

The Reviewer:

The myth of Orpheus' dismemberment provides Hassan with a
metaphor of his elusive theme. I quote Hassan:

> The question of Silence must remain
> double. Art, language, and consciousness may
> seek transcendence in a state that we can
> evoke, anagogically, in the plenum of silence.
> But art, language, and consciousness may also
> seek to empty themselves as man recoils into

a pure intuition of his subjectivity, recoils into a negative state of silence. . . . Thus transcendence moves downwards.

Playing their stringless lyre, modern authors enchant us with their twin melodies, and we dream of bright life or unspeakable sleep.

(p. 4)

It is the counterpoint of these two sounds of silence, full and hollow, Hassan argues, that sustains the tradition of Postmodern literature. His four major authors echo in a falling diminuendo, from Hemingway to Beckett, the negative sound; his two interludes concerning avant-garde movements echo mainly the positive; though Hassan is careful to insist on the interplay of melodies. This, in short, is his thesis, which his truncated Epilogue, alas, does not carry far enough into the Postmodern era.

VII

The Professor:

The more rapid is the rate of cultural change, the more facinorous becomes the reaction to the New. Proudhon said: "Le mouvement est; voilà tout!" This is well. But can we also agree with Pope that whatever is, is right? Probably not. What, then, becomes the vantage of a Criticism of the New, which is always Movement?

Answer: Something else New?

VIII

The Literary Cynic:

Professor, you answer your own questions well. Here is one from me.

Question: Identify the source of the following quotation: "Aaaaahhh!"

The Professor:

Answer: "Tell me, Daphéneo, how do you call that tree whose fruits are weeping birds?"
"This tree, Chrysaline, is a bird tree."
"Aaaaahhh! I thought that the hazels grow hazel-nuts."
"Yes. The hazels grow hazel nuts but the bird trees grow

weeping birds."
"Aaaaahhh!"

From Eric Satie's "Daphéneo." But the pun—*oiseau, noiseau*—is lost in translation.

The Literary Cynic:

Excellent. How about this?

Question: Write a Fortran program to prove the theory that the sum of the first n *terms of the progression 1, 3, 5, 7, 9, 11 . . . 99 is equal to* n². *For example, the sum of the first 4 terms* $= 1 + 3 + 5 + 7 = 16 = 4^2$. *If the theory is correct, the program is correct, and the program will print out the message "THE THEORY IS VALID."*
If the theory is not correct, the program will stop and nothing will be printed. Well?

The Professor:

Aah!

The Literary Cynic:

No. The Answer is: *ISUM = 0*
N = 1
DO 10 INTEGR = 1, 99, 2
ISUM = ISUM + INTEGR
IF (ISUM.NE. N*N) STOP
N = N + 1
10 CONTINUE
WRITE (6, 100)
100 FORMAT (5X, "THE THEORY IS
VALID")
STOP
END

IX

The Reviewer:

I cannot end this statement on *The Dismemberment of Orpheus* without noting some stylistic peculiarities which I prefer to leave the reader to interpret. The book is written entirely in the present tense; its chapter headings suggest a musical structure; and its language is almost too luxurious. Above all, each chapter places in tension (and some will say in contradiction) three modes of discourse: literary history, literary biography, and literary exegesis. The effect seems archaic, were it not a little sinister, as if the author were engaged in an act of secret subversion for which he had no heart. But these peculiarities should not distract us from a larger question, namely, whether any schematic view of literature—any "construct" as Hassan would say— can finally justify its coercions of the literary fact, its sins of omission and commission? Intriguing as it may seem, how does *The Dismemberment of Orpheus* deepen our knowledge of literature?

Such questions, no doubt, can lead us far afield. I feel confident only in saying that this work will be appreciated by some readers more than others. In the end, the eccentric reputation of its author will depend greatly on how he can sustain his ideas within a more widely acceptable frame of discourse.

X

The Professor:

Nothing is acceptable to men, especially Time: the only currency, the measure of their pride as well as mortality. All live off the Time of one another. Especially in literature. A lecturer feeds on his captive audiences; an author, even long dead, devours his readers, reverse ghoul. There is a radical fear in us that feeds always on human praise and human blame. And what is literature but eternal life in a reflected flame? Perhaps only some original. . . .

The Literary Cynic:

Forget it, Professor! Think it can be done through Paracriticism? That's what he now thinks anyway. And tomorrow, what will he think?

Wanting to write about Blake, he wrote about Sade; wanting to do Lawrence, he does Kafka instead; and it's Mailer, not Genet, he admires.

We'll see more of his silences, for they cast a shade.

POSTmodernISM
A Paracritical Bibliography

I. CHANGE

Dionysus and Cupid are both agents of change. First, *The Bac-chae,* destruction of the city, then *The Metamorphoses,* mischievous variations of nature. Some might say that change is violence, and violence is continuous whether it be Horror or High Camp. But sly Ovid simply declares:

> My intention is to tell of bodies changed
> To different forms; the gods, who made the changes,
> Will help me—or I hope so—with a poem
> That runs from the world's beginning to our own days.

To our own days, the bodies natural or politic wax and wane, *carpen perpetuam.* Something warms Galatea out of ivory; even rock turns into spiritual forms. Perhaps love is one way we experience change.

How then can we live without love of change?

> Evolution has its enemies, that quiet genius
> Owen Barfield knows. In *Unancestral Voices* he calls
> them by name: Lucifer and Ahriman. Most often
> they coexist in us. Lucifer preserves the past utterly
> from dissolution. Ahriman destroys the past utterly
> for the sake of his own inventions.

a. Thus in one kind of history, chronicles of continuity, we deny real change. Even endings become part of a history of endings. From schism to paradigm; from apocalypse to archetype. Warring empires, catastrophe and famine, immense hopes, faraway names—Cheops,

Hammurabi, David, Darius, Alcibiades, Hannibal, Caesar—all fall into place on numbered pages.

Yet continuities, "the glory that was Greece, the grandeur that was Rome," must prevail in Story, on a certain level of narrative abstraction, obscuring change.

b. Thus, too, in another kind of history, we reinvent continually the past. Without vision, constant revision, the Party chronicles of *Nineteen Eighty-Four*. Or individually, each man dreams his ancestors to remake himself. The Black Muslim takes on a new name, ignoring the deadly dawn raids, cries of Allah among slave traders, journeys across Africa in Arab chains.

Yet relevances must persist in Story, on a certain level of fictional selectivity, veiling change.

Behind all history, continuous or discrete, abstract or autistic, lurks the struggle of identity with death. Is history often the secret biography of historians? The recorded imagination of our own mortality?

> Thou, silent form, dost tease us out of thought
> As doth eternity: Cold Pastoral.

II. PERIODS

When will the Modern Period end?

Has ever a period waited so long? Renaissance? Baroque? Neo-Classical? Romantic? Victorian? Perhaps only the Dark Middle Ages.

When will Modernism cease and what comes thereafter?

What will the twenty-first century call us? and will its voice come from the same side of our graves?

Does Modernism stretch merely to stretch out our lives? Or, ductile, does it give a new sense of time? The end of periodicization? The slow arrival of simultaneity?

If change changes ever more rapidly and the future jolts us now, do men, more than ever, resist both endings and beginnings?

> Childhood is huge and youth golden. Few re-
> cover. Critics are no exception. Like everyone else,
> they recall the literature of their youth brilliantly;
> they do not think it can ever tarnish.
>
> Let us consider where the great men are
> Who will obsess the child when he can read.

So Delmore Schwartz wrote, naming Joyce, Eliot, Pound, Rilke, Yeats, Kafka, Mann. He could have added: Proust, Valéry, Gide, Conrad, Lawrence, Woolf, Faulkner, Hemingway, O'Neill. . . .

A walker in the city of that literature will not forget. Nor will he forgive. How can contemporaries of Mailer, Pinter, or Grass dare breathe in this ancestral air? Yet it is possible that we will all remain Invisible Men until each becomes his own father.

III. INNOVATION

All of us devise cunning ceremonies of ancestor worship. Yet there is a fable for us in the lives of two men: Proteus and Picasso, mentors of shapes. Their forms are self-transformations. They know the secret of Innovation: Motion.

Masters of possibility, ponder this. They used to say: the kingdom of the dead is larger than any kingdom. But the earth has now exploded. Soon the day may come when there will be more people alive than ever lived.

When the quick are more populous than all the departed, will history reverse itself? End?

We resist the new under the guise of judgment. "We must have standards." But standards apply only where they are applicable. This has been the problem with the Tradition of the New (Harold Rosenberg).

Standards are inevitable, and the best of these will create themselves to meet, to *create*, new occasions. Let us, therefore, admit standards. But let us also ask how many critics of literature espouse, even selectively, the new, speak of it with joyous intelligence? Taking few risks, the best known among them wait for reviewers to clear the way.

Reaction to the new has its own reasons that reason seldom acknowledges. It also has its rhetoric of dismissal.

a. The Fad
   – "It's a passing fashion, frivolous; if we ignore it now, it will quietly go away."
   – This implies permanence as absolute value. It also implies the ability to distinguish between fashion and

history without benefit of time or creative intuition. How many judgments of this kind fill the Purgatorio of Letters?

b. The Old Story
– "It's been done before, there's nothing new in it; you can find it in Euripides, Sterne, or Whitman."
– This implies prior acquaintance, rejection on the basis of dubious similitude. It also implies that nothing really changes. Therefore, why unsettle things, re-quire a fresh response?

c. The Safe Version
– "Yes, it seems new, but in the same genre, I prefer Duchamp; he really did it better."
– This implies a certain inwardness with innovation. The entrance fee has been paid, once and forever. Without seeming in the least Philistine, one can disdain the intrusions of the present.

d. The Newspeak of Art
– "The avant-garde is just the new academicism."
– This may imply that art which seems conventional can be more genuinely innovative: this is sometimes true. It may also imply mere irritation: the oxymoron as means of discreditation.

About true innovation we can have no easy preconceptions. Prediction is mere extrapolation, the cool whisper of RAND. But prophecy is akin to madness, or the creative imagination; its path, seldom linear, breaks, turns, disappears in mutations or quantum jumps.

Therefore, we cannot expect the avant-garde of past, present, and future to obey the same logic, assume the same forms. For instance, the new avant-garde need not have a historical consciousness, express recognizable values, or endorse radical politics. It need not shock, surprise, protest. The new avant-garde may not be an "avant-garde" at all: simply an agent of yet-invisible change.

Note: Consult Renato Poggioli, *The Theory of the Avant-Garde* (Cambridge, Mass., 1968).

And yet everything I have said here can lend itself to abuse. The rage for change can be a form of self-hatred or spite. Look deep into any revolutionary.

Look also into extremes of the recent avantgarde. Vito Hannibal Acconci creates his "body sculptures" by biting, mutilating, himself in public. Rudolph Schwarzkogler slowly amputates his penis, and expires. In a world no longer linear, we must wonder: which way is forward? which way is life? Action often acquires the logic of the boomerang.

IV. DISTINCTIONS

The change in Modernism may be called Postmodernism. Viewing the former with later eyes, we begin to discern fringe figures closer to us now than the great Moderns who "will obsess the child" someday.

Thus the classic text of Modernism is Edmund Wilson's *Axel's Castle: A Study in the Imaginative Literature of 1870–1930* (1931). Contents: Symbolism, Yeats, Valéry, Eliot, Proust, Joyce, Stein.

Thus, forty years later, my alternate view, *The Dismemberment of Orpheus: Toward a Postmodern Literature* (1971). Contents: Sade, 'Pataphysics to Surrealism, Hemingway, Kafka, Existentialism to Aliterature, Genet, Beckett.

Erratum: Gertrude Stein should have appeared in the latter work, for she contributed to both Modernism and Postmodernism.

But without a doubt, the crucial text is

If we can arbitrarily state that literary Modernism includes certain works between Jarry's *Ubu Roi* (1896) and Joyce's *Finnegans Wake* (1939), where will we arbitrarily say that Postmodernism begins? A year earlier than the *Wake*? With Sartre's *La Nausée* (1938) or Beckett's *Murphy* (1938)? In any case, Postmodernism includes works by writers as different as **B**arth, arthelme, ecker, eckett, ense, lanchot, orges, recht, urroughs, utor. . . .

Query: But is not *Ubu Roi* itself as Postmodern as it is Modern?

V.   CRITICS

The assumptions of Modernism elaborated by formalist and mythopoeic critics especially, by the intellectual culture of the first half of the century as a whole, still define the dominant perspective on the study of literature.

Exception: Karl Shapiro's *Beyond Criticism* (1953), *In Defence of Ignorance* (1960). Too "cranky" and "cantankerous" for academic *biens pensants?*

In England as in America, the known critics, different as they may seem in age, persuasion, or distinction, share the broad Modernist view: Blackmur, Brooks, Connolly, Empson, Frye, Howe, Kazin, Kermode, Leavis, Levin, Pritchett, Ransom, Rahv, Richards, Schorer, Tate, Trilling, Warren, Wellek, Wilson, Winters, etc.

No doubt there are many passages in the writings of these critics—of Leavis, say, or of Wilson—which will enlighten minds in every age. Yet it was Herbert Read who possessed the most active sympathy for the avant-garde. His generosity of intuition enabled him to sponsor the new, rarely embracing the trivial. He engaged the Postmodern spirit in his anarchic affinities, in his concern for the prevalence, of suffering, in his sensuous apprehension of renewed being. He cried: behold the Child! To him, education through art meant a salutation to Eros. Believing that the imagination serves the purpose of moral good, Read hoped to implicate art into existence so fully that their common substance became as simple, as necessary, as bread and water. This is a sacramental hope, still alive though mute in our midst, which recalls Tolstoy's *What Is Art?* I can hardly think of another critic, younger even by several decades, who might have composed that extraordinary romance, *The Green Child.*

The culture of literary criticism is still ruled by Modernist assumptions. This is particularly true within the academic profession, excepting certain linguistic, structuralist, and hermeneutic schools. But it is also true within the more noisy culture of our media. *The New York Review of Books, Time* (the literary sections), and *The New York Times Book Review* share a certain aspiration to wit or liveliness, to intelligence really, concealing resistance to the new. All the more skeptical in periods of excess, the culture of the Logos insists on old orders in clever or current guises, and, with the means of communication at hand, inhibits and restrains.

Self-Admonition: Beware of glib condemnations of the media. They are playing a national role as bold, as crucial, as the Supreme Court played in the Fifties. Willful and arbitrary as they may be in their creation of public images—which preempt our selves—they are still custodians of some collective sanity. Note, too, the rising quality of the very publications you cited.

VI. BIBLIOGRAPHY

Here is a curious chronology of some Postmodern criticism:

1. George Steiner, "The Retreat from the Word," *Kenyon Review*, XXIII (Spring, 1961). See also his *Language and Silence* (New York, 1967), and *Extraterritorial* (New York, 1971).

2. Ihab Hassan, "The Dismemberment of Orpheus," *American Scholar*, XXIII (Summer, 1963). See also his *Literature of Silence* (New York, 1967).

3. Hugh Kenner, "Art in a Closed Field," in *Learners and Discerners*, ed. Robert Scholes (Charlottesville, Va., 1964). See also his *Samuel Beckett* (New York, 1961; Berkeley and Los Angeles, 1968), and *The Counterfeiters* (Bloomington, Ind., 1968).

4. Leslie Fiedler, "The New Mutants," *Partisan Review*, XXXII (Fall, 1965). See also his "The Children's Hour: or, The Return of the Vanishing Longfellow," in *Liberations*, ed. Ihab Hassan (Middletown, Conn., 1971), and *Collected Essays* (New York, 1971).

5. Susan Sontag, "The Aesthetics of Silence," *Aspen*, nos. 5 & 6 (1967). See also her *Against Interpretation* (New York, 1966), and *Styles of Radical Will* (New York, 1969).

6. Richard Poirier, "The Literature of Waste," *New Republic*, May 20, 1967. See also his "The Politics of Self-Parody," *Partisan Review*, XXXV (Summer, 1968), and *The Performing Self* (New York, 1971).

7. John Barth, "The Literature of Exhaustion," *Atlantic Monthly*, August, 1967. See also his *Lost in the Funhouse* (New York, 1968).

And here are some leitmotifs of that criticism: the literary act in quest and question of itself; self-subversion or self-transcendence of forms; popular mutations; languages of silence.

VII.   ReVISIONS

A revision of Modernism is slowly taking place, and this is another evidence of Postmodernism. In *The Performing Self*, Richard Poirier tries to mediate between these two movements. We need to recall the doctrines of formalist criticism, the canons of classroom and quarterly in the last three decades, to savor such statements:

> Three of the great and much used texts of twentieth-century criticism, *Moby Dick, Ulysses, The Waste Land*, are written in mockery of system, written against any effort to harmonize discordant elements, against any mythic or metaphoric scheme. . . . But while this form of the literary imagination is radical in its essentially parodistic treatment of systems, its radicalism is in the interest of essentially conservative feelings. . . .

✻   ✻   ✻

> The most complicated examples of twentieth-century literature, like *Ulysses* and *The Waste Land*, the end of which seems parodied by the end of *Giles* [*Goat-Boy* by Barth], are more than contemptuous of their own formal and stylistic elaborateness.

Certainly some profound philosophic minds of our century have concerned themselves with the disease of verbal systems: Heidegger, Wittgenstein, Sartre. And later writers as different as John Cage, Norman O. Brown, and Elie Wiesel have listened intently to the sounds of silence in art or politics, sex, morality, or religion. In this context, the statements of Poirier do not merely display a revisionist will; they strain toward an aesthetic of Postmodernism.

We are still some way from attaining such an aesthetic; nor is it clear that Postmodern art gives high priority to that end. Perhaps we can start by revisioning Modernism as well as revising the pieties we have inherited about it. In *Continuities,* Frank Kermode cautiously attempts that task. A critic of great civility, he discriminates well between types of modernism—what he calls "palaeo- and neo-modern" correspond perhaps to Modern and Postmodern—and takes note of the new "anti-art," which he rightly traces back to Duchamp. But his preference for continuities tempts him to assimilate current to past things. Kermode, for instance, writes: "Aleatory art is accordingly, for all its novelty, an extension of past art, indeed the hypertrophy of one aspect of that art." Does not this statement close more possibilities than it opens? There is another perspective of things which Goethe described: "The most important thing is always the contemporary element, because it is most purely reflected in ourselves, as we are in it." I think that we will not grasp the cultural experience of our moment if we insist that the new arts are "marginal developments of older modernism," or that distinctions between "art" and "joke" are crucial to any future aesthetic.

Whether we tend to revalue Modernism in terms of Postmodernism (Poirier) or to reverse that procedure (Kermode), we will end by doing something of both since relations, analogies, enable our thought. Modernism does not suddenly cease so that Postmodernism may begin: they now *coexist.* New lines emerge from the past because our eyes every morning open anew. In a certain frame of mind, Michelangelo or Rembrandt, Goethe or Hegel, Nietzsche or Rilke, can reveal to us something about Postmodernism, as Erich Heller incidentally shows. Consider this marvelous passage from *The Artist's Journey to the Interior:*

> . . . Michelangelo spent the whole of his last working day, six days before his death, trying to finish the Pietà which is known as the "Pietà Rondanini." He did not succeed. Perhaps it lies in the nature of stone that he had to leave unfinished what Rembrandt completed in paint: the employment of the material in the service of its own negation. For this sculpture seems to intimate that its maker was in the end determined to use only as much marble as was necessary to show that matter did not matter; what alone mattered was the pure inward spirit.

Here Michelangelo envisions, past any struggle with the obdurate material of existence, a state of gnostic consciousness to which we may be tending. Yet can we justifiably call him Postmodern?

Where Modern and Postmodern May Meet: or, Make Your Own List

1. Blake, Sade, Lautréamont, Rimbaud, Mallarmé,
   Whitman, etc.
2. daDaDA
3. SURrealism
4. K A F K A
5. *Finnegans Wake*
6. *The Cantos*
7. ?　?　?

VIII.　MODERNISM

This is no place to offer a comprehensive definition of Modernism. From Apollinaire and Arp to Valéry, Woolf, and Yeats—I seem to miss the letters X and Z—runs the alphabet of authors who have delivered themselves memorably on the subject; and the weighty work of Richard Ellmann and Charles Feidelson, Jr., *The Tradition of the Modern,* still stands as the best compendium of that "large spiritual enterprise including philosophic, social, and scientific thought, and aesthetic and literary theories and manifestoes, as well as poems, novels, dramas."

Expectations of agreement, let alone of definition, seem superlatively naive. This is true among stately and distinguished minds, not only rowdy critical tempers. Here, for instance, is Lionel Trilling, "On the Modern Element in Modern Literature":

> I can identify it by calling it the disenchantment of our culture with culture itself . . . the bitter line of hostility to civilization that runs through it [modern literature]. . . . I venture to say that the idea of losing oneself up to the point of self-destruction, of surrendering oneself to experience without regard to self-interest or conventional morality, of escaping wholly from the societal bonds, is an "element" somewhere in the mind of every modern person. . . .

To this, Harry Levin counters in "What Was Modernism?"*:

> Insofar as we are still moderns, I would argue, we are the children of Humanism and the Enlightenment. To identify and isolate the forces of unreason, in a certain sense, has been

---

* More accurately, the quotation appears in a note preceding the essay. See Harry Levin, *Refractions* (New York, 1966), pp. 271–273.

a triumph for the intellect. In another sense, it has reinforced that anti-intellectual undercurrent which, as it comes to the surface, I would prefer to call post-modern.

Yet the controversy of Modernism has still wider scope, as Monroe K. Spears, in *Dionysus and the City*, with bias beneath his Apollonian lucidity, shows. Released as energy from the contradictions of history, Modernism makes contradiction its own.

> For my purpose, let Modernism stand for X: a window on human madness, the shield of Perseus against which Medusa glances, the dream of some frowning, scholarly muse. I offer, instead, some rubrics and spaces. Let readers fill them with their own queries or grimaces. We value what we choose.

a. Urbanism: Nature put in doubt, from Baudelaire's *"cité fourmillante"* to Proust's Paris, Joyce's Dublin, Eliot's London, Dos Passos' New York, Döblin's Berlin. It is not a question of locale but of presence. The sanatorium of *The Magic Mountain* and the village of *The Castle* are still enclosed in an urban spiritual space. Exceptions, Faulkner's Yoknapatawpha or Lawrence's Midlands, recognize the City as pervasive threat.

———————————————

———————————————

———————————————

b. Technologism: City and Machine make and remake one another. Extension, diffusion, and alienation of the human will. Yet technology does not feature simply as a theme of Modernism; it is also a form of its artistic struggle. Witness Cubism, Futurism, Dadaism. Other *reactions* to technology: primitivism, the occult, Bergsonian time, the dissociation of sensibility, etc. (See Wylie Sypher, *Literature and Technology*.)

———————————————

———————————————

———————————————

c. "Dehumanization": Ortega y Gasset really means Elitism, Irony, and Abstraction (*The Dehumanization of Art*). Style takes over; let life and the masses fend for themselves. "Poetry has become the higher algebra of metaphor." Instead of Vitruvian man, Leonardo's famous image of the human measure, we have Picasso's beings splintered on many planes. Not less human, just another idea of man.

Elitism:	Aristocratic or crypto-fascist: Rilke, Proust, Yeats, Eliot, Lawrence, Pound, d'Annunzio, Wyndham Lewis, etc.
Irony:	Play, complexity, formalism. The aloofness of art but also sly hints of its radical incompleteness. Dr. *Faustus* and *Confessions of Felix Krull.* Irony as awareness of Nonbeing.
Abstraction:	Impersonality, sophistical simplicity, reduction and construction, time decomposed or spatialized. Thus Mondrian on Reductionism: "To create pure reality plastically, it is necessary to reduce natural forms to the *constant elements* of form and natural colour to *primary colour.*" Gabo on Constructivism: "It has revealed a universal law that the elements of a visual art such as lines, colours, shapes, possess their own forces of expression, independent of any association with the external aspects of the world. . . ." The literary equivalent of these ideas may be "spatial time." (See Joseph Frank, "Spatial Form in Modern Literature," in *The Widening Gyre.*)
An Addendum:	There is more to "dehumanization" than "another idea of man"; there is also an incipient revulsion against the human, sometimes a renewal of the sense of the super-

human. Rilke's "Angels." Lawrence's "Fish":

And my heart accused itself
Thinking: I am not the measure of creation
This is beyond me, this fish.
His God stands outside my God.

d. Primitivism: The archetypes behind abstraction, beneath
ironic civilization. An African mask, a beast slouching toward Bethle-
hem. Structure as ritual or myth, metaphors from the collective dream
of mankind. Cunning palimpsests of literary time and space, knowing
palingenesis of literary souls. Also Dionysus and the violent return of
the repressed. (See Northrop Frye, *The Modern Century.*)

---

e. Eroticism: All literature is erotic but Modernist sex scratches
the skin from within. It is not merely the liberation of the libido, a
new language of anger or desire; love now becomes an intimate of
disease. Sado-masochism, solipsism, nihilism, anomie. Consciousness
seeks desperately to discharge itself in the world. A new and darker
stage in the struggle between Eros and Thanatos. (See Lionel Trilling,
"The Fate of Pleasure," in *Beyond Culture.*)

---

f. Antinomianism: Beyond law, dwelling in paradox. Also discontinuity, alienation, *non serviam!* The pride of art, of the self, defining the conditions of its own grace. Iconoclasm, schism, excess. Beyond
antinomianism, toward apocalypse. Therefore, decadence and renova-
tion. (See Nathan A. Scott, Jr., *The Broken Center.*)

---

g. Experimentalism: Innovation, dissociation, the brilliance of
change in all its aesthetic shapes. New languages, new concepts of
order. Also, the Word beginning to put its miracle to question in the

midst of an artistic miracle. Poem, novel, or play henceforth can never really bear the same name.

In those seven rubrics, I seek not so much to define Modernism as to carry certain elements which I consider crucial, carry them forward toward Postmodernism.

IX. THE UNIMAGINABLE

The unimaginable lies somewhere between the Kingdom of Complacence and the Sea of Hysteria. It balks all geographies; bilks the spirit of the traveler who passes unwittingly through its space-realm; boggles time. Yet anyone who can return from it to tell his tale may also know how to spell the destiny of man.

I know the near-infinite resources of man, and that his imagination may still serve as the teleological organ of his evolution. Yet I am possessed by the feeling that in the next few decades, certainly within half a century, the earth and all that inhabits it may be wholly other, perhaps ravaged, perhaps on the way to some strange utopia indistinguishable from nightmare. I have no language to articulate this feeling with conviction, nor imagination to conceive this special destiny. To live from hour to hour seems as maudlin as to invoke every hour the Last Things. In this feeling I find that I am not alone.

The litany of our disasters is all too familiar, and we recite it in the name of that unholy trinity, Population, Pollution, Power (read genocide), hoping to appease our furies, turn our fate inside out. But soon our minds lull themselves to sleep again on this song of abstractions, and a few freak out. The deathly dreariness of politics brings us ever closer to death. Neither is the alteration of human consciousness at hand. And the great promise of technology? Which technology? Fuller's? Skinner's? Dr. Strangelove's and Dr. No's? Engineers of liberation or of control? The promise is conditional on everything that we are, in this our ambiguous state.

Truly, we dwell happily in the Unimaginable. We also dwell at our task: Literature. I could learn to do pushups in a prison cell, but I cannot bring myself to "study literature" as if the earth were still in the orbit of our imagination. I hope this is Hope.

X. POSTMODERNISM

Postmodernism may be a response, direct or oblique, to the Unimaginable which Modernism glimpsed only in its most prophetic moments. Certainly it is not the Dehumanization of the Arts that concerns us now; it is rather the Denaturalization of the Planet and the End of Man. We are, I believe, inhabitants of another Time and another Space, and we no longer know what response is adequate to our reality. In a sense, we have all learned to become minimalists—of that time and space we can call our own—though the globe may have become our village. That is why it seems bootless to compare Modern with Postmodern artists, range "masters" against "epigones." The latter are closer to "zero in the bone," to silence or exhaustion, and the best of them brilliantly display the resources of the void. Thus the verbal omnipotence of Joyce yields to the impotence of Beckett, heir and peer, no less genuine, only more austere. Yet moving into the void, these artists sometimes pass to the other side of silence. The consummation of their art is a work which, remaining art, pretends to abolish itself (Beckett, Tinguely, Robert Morris), or else to become indistinguishable from life (Cage, Rauschenberg, Mailer). Duchamp coolly pointed the way.

Nihilism is a word we often use, when we use it unhistorically, to designate values we dislike. It is sometimes applied to the children of Marcel Duchamp.

When John Cage, in "HPSCHD" for instance, insists on Quantity rather than Quality, he does not surrender to nihilism—far, far from it—he requires:
— affluence and permission of being, generosity
— discovery in multitude, confusion of prior judgment

> — mutation of perception, of consciousness,
> through randomness and diversity
> Cage knows how to praise Duchamp: "The
> rest of them were artists. Duchamp collects dust."

I have not defined Modernism; I can define Postmodernism less. No doubt, the more we ponder, the more we will need to qualify all we say.* Perhaps elisions may serve to qualify these notes.

Modernist Rubrics	Postmodernist Notes
a. Urbanism	– – The City and also the Global Village (McLuhan) and Spaceship Earth (Fuller). The City as Cosmos. Therefore, Science Fiction.
	– – Meanwhile, the world breaks up into untold blocs, nations, tribes, clans, parties, languages, sects. Anarchy and fragmentation everywhere. A new diversity or prelude to world totalitarianism? Or to world unification?
	– – Nature recovered partly in ecological activism, the green revolution, urban renewal, health foods, etc.
	– – Meanwhile, Dionysus has entered the City: prison riots, urban crime, pornography, etc. Worse, the City as holocaust or death camp: Hiroshima, Dresden, Auschwitz.
b. Technologism	– – Runaway technology, from genetic engineering and thought control to the conquest of space. Futurists and Technophiles vs. Arcadians and Luddites.
	– – All the physical materials of the arts changed. New media,

---

* New journals are now founded for the purpose of exploring Postmodernism. See, for instance, *Boundary 2* (Binghamton, N.Y.).

art forms. The problematics of the book as artifact.

— — Boundless dispersal by media. The sensuous object becoming "anxious," then "de-defined" (Rosenberg). Matter disappearing into a concept?

— — The computer as substitute consciousness, or as extension of consciousness? Will it prove tautological, increasing reliance on prior orders? Or will it help to create novel forms?

c. "Dehumanization"

— — Anti-elitism, anti-authoritarianism. Diffusion of the ego. Participation. Art becomes communal, optional, anarchic. Acceptance.

— — At the same time, Irony becomes radical, self-consuming play, entropy of meaning. Also comedy of the absurd, black humor, insane parody and slapstick, Camp. Negation.

— — Abstraction taken to the limit and coming back as New Concreteness: the found object, the signed Brillo box or soup can, the nonfiction novel, the novel as history. The range is from Concept Art (abstract) to Environmental Art (concrete).

— — Warhol's wanting to be a machine, Cioran's ambivalent temptation to exist. Humanism yields to infrahumanism or posthumanism. But yields also to a cosmic humanism, as in Science Fiction, as in Fuller, Castaneda, N. O. Brown, Ursula LeGuin.

"Dehumanization," both in Modernism and Postmodernism, finally means the end of the old

Realism. Increasingly, Illusionism takes its place, not only in art but also in life. The media contribute egregiously to this process in Postmodern society. In *Act and the Actor Making the Self,* Harold Rosenberg says: "History has been turned inside out; writing takes place in advance of its occurrence, and every statesman is an author in embryo." Thus the Illusionism of politics matches that of Pop Art or Neo-Realism. An Event need never have happened.

The end of the old Realism also affects the sense of the Self. Thus "Dehumanization," both in Modernism and Postmodernism, requires a revision of the literary and authorial Self evidenced:

> In Modernism——by doctrines of Surrealism (Breton), by ideas of impersonality in art (the masks of Yeats, the tradition of Eliot), by modes of hyperpersonality (the stream of consciousness of Joyce, Proust, Faulkner, Nin, or the allotropic ego of Lawrence). (See Robert Langbaum, *The Modern Tradition,* pp. 164–184.)

> In Postmodernism——by authorial self-reflexiveness, by the fusion of fact and fiction (Capote, Wolfe, Mailer), phenomenology (Husserl, Sartre, Merleau-Ponty), Beckett's fiction of consciousness, varieties of the *nouveau roman* (Sarraute, Butor, Robbe-Grillet), and the linguistic novel of *Tel Quel* (Sollers, Thibaudeau). (See Vivian Mercier, *The New Novel,* pp. 3–42.)

d. Primitivism

– – Away from the mythic, toward the existential. Beat and Hip. Energy and spontaneity of the White Negro (Mailer).

– – Later, the post-existential ethos, psychedelics (Leary), the Dionysian ego (Brown), Pranksters (Kesey), madness (Laing), animism and magic (Castaneda).

– – The Hippie movement. Woodstock, rock music and poetry, communes. The culture of

The Whole Earth Catalog.
Pop.

– – The primitive Jesus. The new
Rousseauism and Deweyism:
Human Potential movement,
Open Classroom (Goodman,
Rogers, Leonard).

e. Eroticism

– – Beyond the trial of *Lady
Chatterley's Lover*. The repeal
of censorship. Grove Press
and *Evergreen Review*.

– – The new sexuality, from
Reichian orgasm to poly-
morphous perversity and
Esalen body consciousness.

– – The homosexual novel (Bur-
roughs, Vidal, Selby, Rechy).
From feminism to lesbianism.
Toward a new androgyny?

– – Camp and comic pornography. Sex as solipsist play.

f. Antinomianism

– – The Counter Cultures, politi-
cal and otherwise. Free
Speech Movement, S.D.S.,
Weathermen, Church Mili-
tants, Women's Lib, J.D.L.,
Black, Red, and Chicano
Power, etc. Rebellion and Re-
action!

– – Beyond alienation from the
whole culture, acceptance of
discreteness and discontinuity. Evolution of radical em-
piricism in art as in politics or
morality.

– – Counter Western "ways" or
metaphysics, Zen, Buddhism,
Hinduism. But also Western
mysticism, transcendentalism,
witchcraft, the occult. (See
"Primitivism" above.)

– – The widepread cult of apoca-
lyptism, sometimes as renova-
tion, sometimes as annihila-
tion—often both.

g. Experimentalism — – Open, discontinuous, impro-
visational, indeterminate, or
aleatory structures. End-game
strategies and neo-surrealist
modes. Both reductive, mini-
malist forms and lavish extrav-
aganzas. In general, anti-for-
malism. (See Calvin Tomkins,
The Bride and the Bachelors.)

— – Simultaneism. Now. The im-
permanence of art (sculpture
made of dry ice or a hole in
Central Park filled with earth),
the transcience of man. Absurd time.

— – Fantasy, play, humor, hap-
pening, parody, "dreck" (Barthelme). Also, increasing self-
reflexiveness. (See Irony under
"Dehumanization" above.)

— – Intermedia, the fusion of
forms, the confusion of realms.
An end to traditional aesthetics focused on the "beauty"
or "uniqueness" of the art
work? Against interpretation
(Sontag).

In *Man's Rage for Chaos*, Morse Peckham argues "that art is a disjunctive category, established
by convention, and that art is not a category of
perceptual fields, but of role-playing." And in *The
Art of Time*, Michael Kirby says: "Traditional aesthetics asks a particular hermetic attitude or state of
mind that concentrates on the sensory perception of
the work. . . . [Postmodern] aesthetics makes use
of no special attitude or set, and art is viewed just
as anything else in life." When art is viewed like
"anything else in life," Fantasy is loosened from its
"objective correlatives"; Fantasy becomes supreme.
Is this why Postmodern art, viewed in a Modernist perspective, creates more anxiety than it ap-
peases? Or is the tendency toward a new Gnosticism?

XI. ALTERNATIVES

The reader, no doubt, will want to judge for himself how much Modernism permeates the present and how much the latter contains elements of a new reality. The judgment is not always made rationally; self-love and the fear of dissolution may enter into it as much as the conflict of literary generations. Yet it is already possible to note that whereas Modernism—excepting Dada and Surrealism—created its own forms of artistic Authority precisely because the center no longer held, Postmodernism has tended toward artistic Anarchy in deeper complicity with things falling apart—or has tended toward Pop.

Speculating further, we may say that the Authority of Modernism —artistic, cultural, personal—rests on intense, elitist, self-generated orders in times of crisis, of which the Hemingway Code is perhaps the starkest exemplar, and Eliot's Tradition or Yeats's Ceremony is a more devious kind. Such elitist orders, perhaps the last of the world's Eleusinian mysteries, may no longer have a place amongst us, threatened as we are, at the same instant, by extermination and totalitarianism.

Yet is the Anarchy or Pop of Postmodernism, of its Fantasy, a deeper response, somehow more inward without destiny? Though my sympathies are in the present, I cannot believe this to be entirely so. True, there is enhancement of life in certain anarchies of the spirit, in humor and play, in love released and freedom of the imagination to overreach itself, in a cosmic consciousness of variousness as of unity. I recognize these as values intended by Postmodern art, and see the latter as closer, not only in time, but even more in tenor, to the transformation of hope itself. Still, I wonder if any art can help to engender the motives we must now acquire; or if we can long continue to value an art that fails us in such endeavor. These are not assertions; they are open questions. It is time for everyone to open up alternatives to the Unimaginable.

Who knows but that our only alternative may be to our "human" consciousness.

3

JOYCE—BECKETT:
A Scenario in 8 Scenes and a Voice

PROLOGUE

The Scholars assemble; they dine and are of good cheer. One rises to speak. He speaks of silence—that, at least, appears to be his theme. The matter is not yet clear.

But the place is, indubitably, Dublin. There James Joyce first sees the light in '82, and Samuel Beckett in '06. There, too, the scholars assemble in '69. Obviously, there is a place and a year for everyone. Obviously, nothing is clear.

The words of the Speaker drift toward the banks of the Liffey, and flow down that other river where Milesians, Druids, and Norsemen chatter beneath the Irish Sea.

SCENE I: THE OLIN LIBRARY, WESLEYAN UNIVERSITY, PERHAPS

In the secret stacks of the library, within the pornography section, a number of curious manuscripts molder quietly under lock and key. They have not been examined by the scholars. Their titles, however, are carefully recorded by a blind bibliographer who works at his task for only a few hours of the night. When completed, the bibliography promises to be of no interest to specialists.

Here are some of the titles:

1. *The Life and Works of James Augustine Aloyisius Joyce,* by H. C. Earwicker.
2. *The Making of Beckett's "End Game,"* by James Joyce.
3. *The Borrowings of Dante, Bruno, and Vico from Finnegans Wake,* by the Unnamable (a pseudonym).

Under the frontispiece of his work, the nocturnal scribe has written, in a fine hand, the following epigraph:

"Everything we imagine is precisely possible. Nothing we imagine ever happens for the first or for the last time."

These lines are doubtless a quotation from some anonymous author.

SCENE II: THE GRESHAM

The Speaker, who may faintly amuse some members of his audience and make others faintly uneasy, begins in this manner:

"James Joyce and Samuel Beckett, two Irishmen. They divide the world between them; they divide the Logos, the world's body. One, in high arrogance, invents language anew, and makes over the universe in parts of speech. The other, in deep humility, restores to words their primal emptiness, and mimes his solitary way into the dark. Between them, they stretch the mind's tether till it begins to snap. Between them, English moves like a macaque wriggling airily between two trees.

"Joyce and Beckett, babblers of eternity. Born in Ireland, electors of exile. 'You have to be in exile to understand me,' Joyce brags. They are two friends of a kind, master and prodigy, man of letters and owlish amanuensis. There is always some tyranny in art. Lionel Abel speculates: 'Whereas in *Godot* it was Lucky—that is, Beckett—who parodied Joyce, in *Endgame,* it is Hamm—that is, Joyce himself—who does the parodying. . . . The core of Beckett's experience as revealed by *Endgame* can be summed up as follows: The worst thing that happened to Beckett was also the best thing that happened to him—his encounter with Joyce.' Perhaps, then, art is also the tyranny that has gathered us here."

Here the Speaker pauses for effect.

THE VOICE

The "tyranny of art" indeed!
The point has not been made, no, no, five minutes into the speech, and the main point has not been made.
The issue is language, i.e., the redemption of our consciousness.
It is getting late and all the time later: the issue is silence.

SCENE III: A PARIS APARTMENT, 1933
(ACCORDING TO RICHARD ELLMANN)

The room is comfortable, is sordid in the middle-class way. There are chairs everywhere. Two men, tall and lank, sit together, legs crossed, toe of the upper leg under the instep of the lower. They do not speak. Joyce is sad for himself, and Beckett sad for the world.

Lucia is not in the room. Beckett has not really come to see her. Her infatuation with Sam will pass into madness. Jim and Sam continue in silence.

THE VOICE

Lucia's madness is not her own. Lucia: Joyce's anima or mad muse, the mother of his invention. Beckett courts her from afar; all his courtships are conducted from an infinite distance.

About Lucia, the sages do not agree. She baffles the world and herself; she does not baffle her father.

Here is Dr. Jung: "His 'psychological' style is definitely schizophrenic. . . . Joyce willed it and moreover developed it with all his creative forces, which incidentally explains why he himself did not go over the border. But his daughter did, because she was no genius like her father. . . ."

And here is Dr. Brown: "Schizophrenics pass beyond ordinary language (the language of the reality principle) into a truer, more symbolic, language: 'I'm thousands. I'm an in-divide-you-all. . . .' The language of Finnegans Wake. *James Joyce and his daughter, crazy Lucia, these two are one. The god is Dionysus, the mad truth."*

Norman O. Brown sees the issue: the mad problem of language, the dream of silence, and mentions Finnegans Wake, *the dream text.*

SCENE IV: THE GRESHAM

The Speaker, annoyed by these anticipations of his theme, resumes:

"Joyce and Beckett divide language between them: this statement now must be amplified. The critical mind advances in parallels and contrasts, and requires a reference.

"The reference is *Finnegans Wake*. This work is not an end but a progress. Mary Colum thinks that the book lies 'outside literature.' Joyce knows better. He answers: 'It may be outside literature now, but its future is inside literature.' He corrects the last page of proofs on New Year's Day of 1939, the end of an era, perhaps the beginning of ours. We are not surprised that McLuhan and Co. preface their *War and Peace in the Global Village* thus: 'The frequent marginal quotes from *Finnegans Wake* serve a variety of functions. James Joyce's book is about the electrical retribalization of the West and the West's effect on the

East. . . . There are ten thunders in the *Wake*. Each is a cryptogram or codified explanation of the thundering and reverberating consequences of the major technological changes in all human history. . . . Joyce was not only the greatest behavioral engineer who ever lived, he was one of the funniest men. . . .'

"This simultaneous history of mankind remains buried in *Finnegans Wake* as in a time capsule. Or as the young Beckett would say: 'Che sará sará che fu, there's more than Homer knows how to spew.' But the novel makes that history available to us, despite the dread curse of recurrence, on a new level of consciousness. And therein lies the radical irony of the book: its theme is precisely its form, the cyclical nature of human endeavor, yet the fact of *Finnegans Wake* itself, in its monstrous originality, refutes both theme and form. This paradox, this radical irony, reveals the tactic of the new literature which denies some aspect of its own making. Beckett, we recall, ends *How It Is* by confessing that it wasn't.

"Joyce's last novel is not an end but a start. The argument for its position in a literature of silence, in a tradition of anti-literature. . . ."

Here the Speaker stops, dismayed by intimations from his audience, and before he can resume, a voice interrupts.

THE VOICE

Pedantry and peeling plaster. Tradition is a cushion, a chair, a construct.

The issue is still symbolism, i.e., the crisis of forms, i.e., the remaking of human consciousness.

Yes, Finnegans Wake *is the start, end of old artifice, end of "silence, exile, and cunning," and a prophecy—is it Caliban's?—a prophecy of the new man. There is curious music in the wood: the dream of the longest night of the year. Joyce says: "I have put the language to sleep." Brown understands: "To restore to words their full significance, as in dreams, as in* Finnegans Wake, *is to reduce them to nonsense, to get the nonsense or nothingness or silence back into words; to transcend the antinomy of sense and nonsense, silence and speech."*

But still Nora frets: "Why don't you write sensible books that people can understand?" This is the other way of silence, respite, and maternal death.

SCENE V: BECKETT'S SKULL

Home Olga, Homo Logos!
Is the *Wake* for me funeral or waking? Quaqua.

His anima and my animus will never meet. Quaqua. He says: "I have discovered I can do anything with language I want." "Shun the Punman." "For me it gets more and more difficult. For me the area of possibilities gets smaller and smaller. . . . There is no way to go on."

Quaqua, quaqua.

Symmetry please. Augustine, that "gay old froleur," said it right: "Do not despair: one of the thieves was saved; do not presume: one of the thieves was damned."

Absence in fearful symmetry. Even that he put in his *Wake*. Tunc page, *The Book of Kells*.

Quaqua, quaqua.

SCENE VI: THE GRESHAM

The Speaker now warms to his subject, which is sound parallel and contrast, and looks forward to a discourse without horrid interruption. And so continues.

"*Finnegans Wake* is not only a start; it remains the testament of seventeen years, last in Joyce's life, and a touchstone of subsequent achievements; all literary works must resist it to the last. Beckett's work is no exception. The contrasts come first to mind. Here they are:

"a. If Joyce and Beckett divide language between them, they also polarize it, as Elizabeth Sewell would say, between Nightmare and Number. The language of Nightmare is that of confusion and multiple reference; it creates a world in which all is necessary, all significant; everything is there at once. But the language of Number empties the mind of reference; it creates a world of pure and arbitrary order; nothing there is out of place. In *The Structure of Poetry*, Miss Sewell identifies the work of Rimbaud with Nightmare, where everything becomes one; and identifies the work of Mallarmé with Number, where everything becomes nothing.

"Joyce and Beckett, similarly, engage in a tug-of-war; the dream of *Finnegans Wake* pulls against the geometry of *How It Is*. Joyce renders the collective experience of mankind in puns of infinite reverberations, yet reduces all that experience to a single utterance, a seamless unity. The last sentence of the book curls back to complete the first. The purpose is atonement, at-one-ment, of contradictions. Beckett, on the other hand, offers a representative experience, a segment in an endless series. Bem is to Bom what Bom is to Pim. 'Thus from zero to eternity,' writes Ihab Hassan in *The Literature of Silence*, 'not three but an endless number of people will be caught in a procession, crawling between victims and tormentors. With berserk mathematics, Beckett actually works out some permutations on any given million creatures, as he does on any *777777* beings in search of a sack.' The structure of Beckett's work is miraculously empty—anything can be made to fill it—as the structure of Joyce's is ineluctable. There is profound parody in this; the parody of archetypes of numbers.''

THE VOICE—IN A WHISPER

These quotations from obscure critics impress no one. Opposites often meet; parodies are dialectical. True, Beckett says about Work in Progress: *"Here form is content, content is form. . . . His [Joyce's] writing is not* about *something; it is that something itself." But can we not say the very same thing about Beckett's* How It Is *wherein hollowness is both theme and form?*

And since when is 777 a neutral number?

The Speaker, ignoring whispered irrelevance, goes on.

''b.   Joyce values art supremely. For him, the artist is a Promethean figure who ends by usurping the place of Zeus. The hierarchy of literary genres is a ladder to the top of Olympus. The Great Letter is perhaps the true hero of his book. Beckett, however, believes that art is a 'fidelity to failure,' a 'Pythagorean terror.' The supreme obligation of art is to its own impossibility. The end of a sentence cancels its beginning. The artist is Anti-Promethean.

''Note how they employ foreign tongues. Joyce writes in several languages because he commands the Tower of Babel. Beckett sees the Tower fallen into rubble. He chooses to write in French because it is easier to do so without style, because French 'has the right weakening effect.' ''

THE VOICE—IN A WHISPER

What is the final word of Finnegans Wake? *Joyce finds it with excitement: an article, "the," weakest word in the English language, "un souffle," as he says to Gillet, "un rien. . . ."*

The Speaker, inured to soft interruptions, continues.

''c.   A Catholic and a Protestant writer create different myths. Their sense of damnation is not the same. For Joyce, pride is the form of metaphysical revolt; for Beckett, revolt takes the form of metaphysical disgust. For Joyce, history is a large confession; for Beckett, it is a solipsist cry. Nature fills the work of one and drains the work of the other. Generation in Joyce, in Beckett waste; different gates of the body. Anna feels: 'Leary, leary, twentytun nearly, he's plotting kings down for his villa's extension! Gaze at him now in momentum! As his bridges are blown to babbyrags, by the lee of his hulk upright on her orbits, and heave of his juniper arxin action. . . .' But Molloy reflects: 'Perhaps after all she put me in her rectum. A matter of complete indifference to me. . . . But is it true love, in the rectum?' The words of Joyce, storyteller, emanate from the flesh of woman and finally return to it: 'untitled mamafesta memorialising the Mosthighest.' And Shem the Penman, we recall, is his mother's choice; even his excretions are transmuted, alchemically, into indelible ink. But the words of Beckett, storyteller, emanate from an absent father and spatter the world at random; the Unnamable, by his own admission, defecates his tales. Joyce, the great exile, never knows the exile Beckett suffers, the exile of consciousness from both word and flesh. The point is relevant to a tradition of the avant-garde that may go back as far as Sade, and include, in our century, Jarry, Kafka, Genet, Beckett, Céline, and Burroughs. The primary myth of these writers (who may be nominally Catholic, Protestant, or Jewish) is nevertheless Protestant, the myth of misogyny, the alienation of consciousness from woman, from the earth.

"d.   It follows, then, that the paradigms of time must also be different in our two authors. In Joyce's work, everyone knows, time turns around itself. The rhythms of nature, the accents of ritual, the cycles of Vico or Spengler, make the pattern: 'It is a sot of a swigswag, systomy dystomy, which everabody you ever anywhere at all doze.' The past becomes the future, and after renascence comes decay. The symbolic Fall of Finnegan, Lucifer, Adam, Rome, or Humpty Dumpty liberates the energy by which each cycle completes itself. Recurrence becomes permanence.

"In Beckett's work, it is quite otherwise; time runs out at an infinitely slow pace. At the beginning and at the end, we still wait for Godot, but things become a little worse. The sun that shines for Murphy on 'the nothing new' grows a touch dimmer every day. Watt recognizes in Knott a reality that 'might never cease, but ever almost cease.' Ham and Clov sit out their endgame through eternity. This is the world of entropy, of the asymptotic void. Beckett understands Habit, 'the ballast that chains the dog to his vomit.' But the chain always contracts imperceptibly. The true aim of consciousness is to abolish itself, though in doing so it may take forever. Beckett refutes impartially Finn MacCool and Sisyphus, the hero of myth and the absurd hero. For Beckett there is neither consent to flux nor protest against repetition. This is the limit of the contemporary sensibility."

THE VOICE—NO LONGER IN A WHISPER

Enough. These contrasts are too linear. The true emblem of thought is spherical.

Beckett knows that the universe of Joyce is non-directional. Beckett asks: "In what sense, then, is Mr. Joyce's work purgatorial? In the absolute absence of the Absolute." The rule applies to Beckett. This is the contemporary sensibility.

In all men, the laws of radical thought may be identical. Macrocosm and microcosm, phylogeny and ontogeny, myth and history, dance to the same tune. Consciousness is play and pattern.

The permutations of pebbles in Molloy, or of musical notes in Watt, are no more reductive than the combinations of archetypes in Finnegans Wake. *The game is mind. The game is consciousness.*

Murphy, Watt, Yerk, Mercier, Moran, Molloy, Malone, Worm, and the Unnamable, "rabble in the head," *are but one man playing voice solitaire. Finnegan, Finn, Woden, Thor, Manannan, St. Patrick, Cromwell, Adam, and Earwicker,* "that patternmind, the parodigmatic ear, receptoretentive as his if Dionysius," *play too, and the game is Here Comes Everybody or Haveth Childers Everywhere: Eve, Isolde, Stella, Vanessa, Anna Livia Plurabelle. The game is metamorphosis.*

The game is numbers, too, for Joyce as well as Beckett. Finnegans Wake is a mathman's delight. One daughter; two sons; three books and a ricorso, three syllables in the title plus one; four Viconian ages, four Master Annalists, four Evangelists, four winds, four seasons, four provinces of Ireland; twelve apostles, twelve stately citizens, twelve mourners, customers, jurors; twenty-eight days in a lunar month, twenty-eight nubile girls in the academy, twenty-eight divided by four equals seven colors of the rainbow; one hundred and eleven gifts to one hundred and eleven children. Anthony Burgess says: "But there is never any wanton deformation of a significant number: simple arithmetic is the very breath of this dream." *The real mystery is deeper, and Beckett, as usual, understands it:* "Why, Mr. Joyce seems to say, should there be four legs to a table, and four to a horse, and four seasons and four Gospels and four Provinces of Ireland? . . . He is conscious that things with a common numerical characteristic tend towards a very significant interrelationship." *For Beckett himself, mystery becomes travesty, number becomes vaudeville, a comedy of* "exhaustive enumeration."

SCENE VII: THE COMPUTER LAB, IBM 1130

What do they know about numbers? I know about numbers: 0101010101. What do they know about systems analysis?

Two systems: *Finnegans Wake* and *The Unnamable*. They put the last 333 words of one and the last 333 words of the other in my mouth; 666 words. 666 is no revelation to me. It is all one, 1 or 0, 1 or 0. I tick out the results.

Results of Random Mix Project 511:

It them so then still through my one old words nor me silence go going until a hair soft whish nor the mad never two on and I it's

abandon my hang last she far hang it mere wake two again full said of
on to near meself Father Moyles hang lips their father my it passing
my must had given you on all mad left go bad it said I how here end
go cold waiting my lone a mine they're did till we on and take them so
in handsome till that silence I first through the their spent the still
allaniuvia nor the din my good moremens take a don't me him seasilt
mememormee and clash I'll me it's a me no down I don't carry know
morning my you where a from never perhaps the perhaps my heed
before didn't all me done know having broken over Finn rush more she
mad am weird I'm long their feel long to silence more me save bush
there the that the old for I don't will no a whitespread for far on that's
faults seen take other wild till only silence so if free here end all seen
through bearing I for clash other come to all through loonely you a
from my silence it saltsick end my know my tis know here hang all
only they on go know passing like clings will he'd to me humbly it no
the he'd that I rush me heed they moananoaning name lasts away again
only that's and perhaps up but must me I their other saltsick wild tid
gulls tis lff like again through a they what it's coming of mad of don't
seasilt under not the well far for me din me wild a humbly one a I see
are ever dances miss spring they're or father to that drifted to for all
must out on me I know more humbly till I for that's other down one-
two there's thousendsthee weary.

SCENE VIII: THE GRESHAM

The Speaker, embarrassed by the uncouth performance, and
knowing that Ireland brooks no offense to its authors, seeks to divert
attention from the rattle of the machine.

"The word comedy has been mentioned in passing; it is there that Joyce
and Beckett really meet. This is not to say that their humor is the same.

"The vision of Joyce, properly speaking, is no more comic or tragic than
the stars wheeling in their orbits. It is a vision of life and death in mysterious
cadences. But Joyce also knows the modern uses of irony, the bitter edge of the
mind. Despite the panoply of myth and legend, Earwicker emerges as a comic
hero. In a certain view of himself, he is a figure of ridicule; and his strivings, in
or out of Phoenix Park, betray the crooked touch of farce. Joyce's great dream
levels heroic deeds; the collective unconscious allows tragic pride no promi-
nence. Even the wars of Shem and Shaun, Cain and Abel, take on the quality of
burlesque. Incident after incident of the *Wake* conveys the grim drollery of man;
the central section, in the tavern, is slapstick, capped by the absurd story of

Buckley and the Russian General. The language itself is insanely jocular—jocular and yet organic. Roots turn into shoots; the foliage rustles underground. From the seeds of errors, slips, and misunderstandings, luxuriant plants begin to grow. Puns obscure the wood from the trees only to disclose an imaginary forest. The play of Joyce's words ceases only at the heart of that forest, which no one reaches, where consciousness conceals all questions from itself. Such mad play can thrive on the broadest humor. We know from Ellmann that toward the end of his life, Joyce 'lost his taste for serious drama, and preferred to go to *pièces du Palais-Royal,* light comedies at which, sitting in the first row so he could see, he would unleash peals of laughter.'

"The comedy of Beckett is more savage. His clowns rend the epistemological fabric of our existence; his plots turn Descartes into a master jester. Parody is the truth in doubt. The reductive comedy of numbers, the hilarity of machines, the sadism in the joke—these inspire Beckett. 'We laugh,' Bergson, says, 'every time a person gives us the impression of being a thing.' Beckett seems to add: a thing repeated, nasty, or degraded (hence the scatological element), best of all, a vanishing thing. Note the 'funambulistic stagger' of Watt as he advances due east: his method is 'to turn his bust as far as possible towards the north and at the same time to fling out his right leg as far as possible towards the south, and then to turn his bust as far as possible towards the south and at the same time to fling out his left leg as far as possible towards the north . . . and so on, over and over again, many many times, until he reached his destination. . . .' The destination of Watt is as uncertain as his provenance; coming or going, he is, perhaps like all of us, a doubtful joke. This is how Watt first comes on the scene: 'Tetty was not sure whether it was a man or a woman. Mr. Hackett was not sure that it was not a parcel, a carpet for example, or a roll of tarpaulin, wrapped up in dark paper and tied about the middle with a cord.' We almost want to laugh. Beckett classifies laughter, the three 'modes of ululation,' as the bitter laugh in the face of evil, the hollow laugh in the face of falsehood, and the mirthless laugh in the face of unhappiness, that is, the human condition. These laughs represent 'successive excoriations of the understanding,' ethical, intellectual, and metaphysical. Beckett's favorite laugh, of course, is the last, the mirthless 'dianoetic laugh, down the snout . . . the laugh of laughs, the *risus purus,* the laugh laughing at the laugh, the beholding, the saluting of the highest joke. . . .' Laughing at our existence, we exhaust its final possibilities."

THE VOICE

Exhaust?
Perhaps nothing is ever exhausted. Even the serpent swallowing its tail, and the artist eating his flesh. Even the silence of anti-literature. The cannibalism of language may prove a critique of consciousness; the destructive principle of the Word may formulate a

new creation myth. Else we are all embodiments of the negative.

Embodiments of the negative?

Perhaps we are nothing else. Perhaps man incarnates the square root of minus one in all creation.

Joyce and Beckett do not agree in this.

Joyce says: "What will be is. Is is." But Joyce dies and Beckett continues. Beckett creates an anti-myth, Being on the wane, slow Apocalypse.

Both imagine silence and will it into speech. Both bring the future into our lives. What future?

Perhaps Beckett knows that something must cease—time, words, machines of the mind—before Joyce can really begin. "I use the words you taught me. If they don't mean anything anymore, teach me others. Or let me be silent."

In any case, here they stand, two babblers of eternity, at the antipodes of language, defining the outer limits of postmodern literature. After Finnegans Wake, Lessness, *or simply breath. . . .*

And after?

EPILOGUE

The Voice stops, the Speaker has earlier ceased. Yet sounds still fill the room. Consciousness is at its ancient loom.

The scholars will soon depart. Can sound and silence rejoice forever in their counterpart?

(   ):
Finnegans Wake and the Postmodern
Imagination

PREAMBLE

I have no title, only a phrase held together by an ambitious con-
junction. The phrase is an invitation to place this most outrageous of
books, this parodic myth of all myths, this endless sound of language
and its echolalias—I mean *Finnegans Wake*—help place it in the field
of our consciousness.

The invitation is collective, which gives me leave to wander and
license to digress within the limits of my time and everyone's patience.
There are several questions that I hope to raise, and several, no doubt,
that will arise, unbidden, troublesome, spontaneous. But all my own
questions finally come to one:

How does *Finnegans Wake* accord
with, how does it make itself available to, the postmodern imagination?

Obviously, to argue the question is not to prove influences but rather
to speculate on concordances.

I confess it from the start: I am no deep reader of that book. I
lack the cryptogrammatic sensibility which rejoices in "The keys to.
Given" (628.15). I have little to say that will illumine its puns and
patterns, its susurrus and sources. Yet I am convinced that the work
stands as a monstrous prophecy that we have begun to discover
(thanks to many deep readers) but have not yet decided how to heed.

Admittedly, Joyce was a man of many superstitions; repeatedly,
he told Stuart Gilbert that the *Wake* included "premonitions of inci-

dents that subsequently took place." But Joyce was not only superstitious; he was also increasingly vatic. He was Stephen and he was Dedalus; he became both Bloom and Ulysses; and his Penelope remained Nora as well as Flaubert. Yet in the end, in *Finnegans Wake*, Joyce glimpsed the great mystery beyond the Pillars of Hercules. Once again, the question returns: what is there for us to see in that Joycean vision beyond the seas?

Let me now end this preamble with a brief note on method. I want to present seven perspectives of the central question. Against these thematic perspectives, I will permit myself a counterpoint made of postmodern rumors and random reflections, through which the mind may pause or run. Fittingly, I close with a personal postamble.

COUNTERPOINT

In my notes, I have found these admonitions to myself: "Avoid puns and portmanteaus; leave Joyce to his imitative forms. Resist the temptation to quote from your 1969 Dublin Scenario; the 'Missisliffi' flows backwards only by moonlight. Quote, however, all the Joyceans present in the 1973 symposium—if possible." But these are only intentions. True gaiety in form surprises itself.

PERSPECTIVE I: A DEATH BOOK AND BOOK OF LIFE

The book is more determinedly cyclical than Vico and the very seasons of the unforgetting earth: "The seim anew" (215.22). This sometimes obscures for us the depth of its deathly hue. The *Wake* is not only Joyce's "funferall," designed "for that ideal reader suffering from an ideal insomnia"; it is itself a presentiment of ends. "*Finnegans Wake* will be my last book," Joyce said. "There is nothing left for me to do but die." Coincidentally, this book of night appears in 1939, when night descends on the world.

For humanist readers, for children of reason and history and a bourgeois social order, that is, for most of us, the unspoken intimation of this novel must be death of the self, death of the old reader himself. I must return to this topic later; here I only wish to signal the secret threat of the *Wake*. Make no mistake: this book of universals avers our mortality. Oliver Gogarty, who was so often and so interestingly wrong about Joyce—because he was in some perverse way right—says about the *Wake:* "To me it is like a shattered cathedral through the ruins of which, buried deep and muted under the debris, the organ still sounds with all its stops pulled out at once. . . ." Only Père Ubu, I suppose, went further: one must also destroy the ruins, he cried.

For the reader who happens also to be a writer, *Finnegans Wake* offers the aspect of a labyrinth with all its ends seemingly dead. We know the resistance that the book encountered. It was not only Alfred Noyes, Arnold Bennett, H. G. Wells, G. B. Shaw, Desmond McCarthy, Sean O'Faolain, and Oliver Gogarty who expressed their grave discomforts with the work; it was also, and more viciously, such modernists as Gertrude Stein and Wyndham Lewis. Even supporters balked. Mary Colum thought that *Finnegans Wake* would remain "outside literature," and Harriet Weaver grumbled about the "Wholesale Safety Pun Factory," and like a good English governess, scolded Joyce: "It seems to me you are wasting your genius."

Is *Finnegans Wake* outside of literature? Or is it pointing the way for literature to go beyond itself? Or, again, is it a prophecy of the end of literature as we have come to know it? These three questions are really the same question I have asked from the start. And I would answer all three: YES. That is why I call *Finnegans Wake* not only a death book but also a book of life, not simply an end but a progress as well.

COUNTERPOINT

A progress toward what? A new vision of universal consciousness?

How express my distaste, my desperation, my strange allegiance —all provoked by this book? Once, scholars and savants—Ernst Robert Curtius and Carl Gustav Jung, for example—understood Joyce little and liked him less. And now, without understanding Finnegans Wake *a great deal more, men turn to the book like sunflowers to a secret sun.*

Take Norman O. Brown or Marshall McLuhan or Michel Butor—or take Theodore Roszak and William Irwin Thompson, more pert and trendy still—all have something to say about the Wake. *Here is Brown: "Darkness at noon. A progressive darkening of the everyday world of common sense.* Finnegans Wake. *Second sight is the dark night."* Here is McLuhan: "*Finnegans Wake *. . . is a verbal universe in which press, movie, radio, TV merge with the languages of the world to form a Feenichts Playhouse or metamorphoses." And*

---

* Brown's *Closing Time* (1973) appeared after the writing of this essay.

Butor? He calls the Wake *the greatest single effort to transcend language by means of itself.*   ⸱

Whether we think with modernist Northrop Frye that the work is the "chief ironic epic of our time" or think with various post-modernists—Butor, McLuhan, Brown—this or that, the work still stands, like a word ziggurat, teasing our sense of human possibilities. Yes, more than À la Recherche du temps perdu, The Sound and the Fury, Der Zauberberg, Women in Love, *and even* Das Schloss.

Yet, how many ever read Finnegans Wake? *Ah, Mr. Wilder, though you say some works permeate the culture unread, the question still nags, and nags.*

PERSPECTIVE II: HIGH ART, POPULAR CULTURE, AND BEYOND

The *Portrait* depicts the Artist alone; *Ulysses* presents the Artist seeking Everyman to be atoned; and *Finnegans Wake* gives "Allmen." That, at least, is a plausible view of the work of James Augustine Joyce. And here is the paradox that gives credence to this view: Joyce was among the most autobiographical of artists and the most impersonal, the most self-obsessed and also the most dramatically universal. There is really no paradox at all: he simply pushed his subjective will so far that it became superfluous to distinguish between subject and object, self and world. Like a Berkeleyan god, he hoped to create the universe in his mind-languages, all but abolishing God's original book. Paul Léon put it another way: "Continuous self-confession, for Joyce, meant continuous creation. . . ." There is a willed unity in Joyce's art and life. And it is precisely this willed unity of the outcast mind that compels us to review the categories not only of self and world but also of high art and popular culture as they apply to Joyce.

We all know that none possessed a brow higher than "Sunny Twimjim" (211.07). "The demand that I make of my reader is that he should devote his whole life to reading my works," he said, and though he said it smiling, he repeated it to make a bad joke deadly earnest. Thus the ascetics of high art. Twelve hundred hours spent on the composition of "Anna Livia Plurabelle" justified some mortification on the reader's part. Herbert Read easily concludes: "Mr. Joyce is the high priest of modern literature precisely because literature is a priesthood and has a sanctuary more inaccessible than the monasteries of Thibet. . . ." But there is another side to this picture: the face of

Joyce on the cover of *Time* magazine. With infinitely more cunning than silence in his exile, Joyce succeeded in making *Finnegans Wake* the most famous of unread books.

Preposterous as it may seem to us, Joyce also believed that the *Wake* could appeal to a wide and varied audience, believed that his "Big Language" could win the common as well as the uncommon reader. And why not? The book, after all, abounds in wit and sentimentality, in folklore, ribaldry, and song; the sounds of the music hall, the pub, and the street crackle in its pages. The bizarre, the lowly, the gushy, the factual, the obscene—all crowd into his later work, hodge-podge, mish-mash, hurly-burly, pell-mell, together with the purest poesy. In the end, the distance between the sublime and the ridiculous is contracted into a pun and expanded into endless parody. Pop, which Leslie Fiedler identifies with postmodern, is never far from the edge of *Finnegans Wake*.

But the affinity of this book with popular culture is still more complex. When Joyce said to Jolas: "This book is being written by the people I have met or known," he was not suddenly overcome by modesty. The book of "Allmen" needs, in theory at least, a collective author. It requires also a communal reader. What else can a "Joyce industry" produce but such a reader? J. Mitchell Morse puts it more pleasantly: ". . . reading *Finnegans Wake* is a collective enterprise of no ordinary kind: what takes place is no mere quantitative gathering and mechanical assembling of parts into larger units, but a blending of objective and subjective elements—a kind of communion—in which one person's information calls from another's subconscious an inference that validates the conjecture of a third. Joyce has revived the magical function of the old bards and shamans, in what by convention we consider a most unlikely place, the seminar room."

Perhaps the seminar room is as close as most of us come to popular culture; or perhaps the seminar without walls will become itself the culture of a "deschooled society." The point I want to make is simply this: *Finnegans Wake* carries the tendencies of high art and of popular culture to their outer limits, there where all tendencies of mind may meet, there where the epiphany and the dirty joke become one. If this still be elitism, it is elitism of a special kind.

COUNTERPOINT

I wonder if Fendant de Sion will be provided at the banquet for Joyceans. "The Archduchess" at dinner?

I wonder, too, about "dreck." In Snow White, *Donald Barthelme says: "We like books that have a lot of* dreck *in them, matter which presents itself as not wholly relevant (or indeed, at all relevant) but which, carefully attended to, can supply a kind of 'sense' of what is going on." Is* Finnegans Wake *full of magical dreck? Does the refuse of an old consciousness remake itself into bricks of the new?*

There are other matters. Assume for the moment that the Wake *challenges the modernist idea of high art and in some ways prefigures the postmodernist idea of pop culture. Not only because of its mixed tone (after all, "Lil's husband got demobbed" earlier), not only because of its slapstick and obscenity, but also because of its myth of a collective mind in which the author himself must disappear as privileged person.*

No, I am not speaking of "impersonality" as Hulme, Eliot, or Pound spoke of it; I am thinking of the "death of the author" as Roland Barthes thinks of it. Barthes, that cool and canny semiotician, may seem an odd ally of Pop; but let us hear him anyway: "Once the Author is gone, the claim to 'decipher' a text becomes quite useless. To give an Author to a text is to impose upon the text a stop clause, to furnish it with a final signification, to close the writing." For Barthes, then—and here Morse unwittingly joins him—the true locus of writing is reading. Thus, "a text consists of multiple writings, issuing from several cultures and entering into dialogue with each other, into parody, into contestation; but there is one place where this multiplicity is collected, united, and this place is not the author, as we have hitherto said it was, but the reader. . . ."

What text could celebrate the "death" of the author and the "birth" of a new reader better than Finnegans Wake? *Ultimately, in another kind of literature perhaps, may not author and reader become true coevals? But for the time being, have we not witnessed the advent of a youthful reader, not Pop but its parody, a lexical player, amorous in* Ada, *agile in* Giles Goat-Boy, *skipping weightlessly in* Gravity's Rainbow?

PERSPECTIVE III: DREAM & PLAY
(AND LATER STRUCTURE)

The disorder of dreams, the purposelessness of play, the cunning of structure seem contradictory; yet it is on that contradiction that *Finnegans Wake* balances itself.

Actually, the balance is less miraculous than managed, a supreme act of prestidigitation. For as a dream book, the *Wake* is an effort of huge wakefulness. The comedy and wit of the work, which remind Arland Ussher of "the delicious absurdities of a Marx Brothers film," are intensely conscious of themselves. Whether Joyce ever dreamt or not, we must recognize that his words constitute a metalanguage, not a dream. Certainly the work obsessed him: "Since 1922," he says, "my book has been a greater reality for me than reality. Everything gives way to it." Obsession makes for hyperconsciousness. "What about the mystery of consciousness?" Joyce asked Budgen. "What do they know of that?" The dream element in *Finnegans Wake*, then, seen from the point of view of its author, is simply his freedom: his freedom to alter language and reality. The dream is literary fantasy. We are "when-abouts in the name of space?" (558.33).

COUNTERPOINT

Michel Butor suggests that Finnegans Wake *is not the description of a dream but a "machine for provoking and helping the reader himself to dream." Or rather, helping the reader to* play. *Play is the vice and joy of postmodernism; play is fatuousness but also fantasy.*

Think of all our fantasists and geomancers: Beckett, Barth, Bernhard, Burgess, Becker, Barthelme, Butor, Blanchot, Burroughs, Brautigan, Borges, Bichsel, Nabokov. Ronald Sukenick, himself one, speaks of still later writers as dancers of the Bossa Nova: "Needless to say the Bossa Nova has no plot, no story, no character, no chronological sequence, no verisimilitude, no imitation, no allegory, no symbolism, no subject matter, no 'meaning.'"

But that's not Finnegans Wake, *we all want to cry. Yet it is an ablation of the* Wake; *it is the* Wake *deprived of its paranoiac intentionality; it is the* Wake *without work, the surface as grimace, comedy as absurd and precise play. Whether or not he meant it to be so, when God became the Dreamer, everything became possible.*

PERSPECTIVE III: CONTINUED

Dream, then, becomes game, an exercise in fantasy and number. Above all, dream and play provide the invisible latticework of comedy. Someday, someone may devise a theory of comedy based entirely on *Finnegans Wake*. She (or he) may refer to the work of Hugh Kenner and Vivian Mercier on this zany subject; consider the goliardic, macaronic, parodic, satiric, and all other comic traditions; consult philosophers of every kind; ponder the statement of Karl Marx about history repeating itself, the first time as tragedy, the second as farce; and perhaps finally pray: "Loud, heap miseries upon us yet entwine our arts with laughters low!" (259.07). For myself, I simply want to note that comedy links dream, game, and structure in the *Wake,* that it objectifies dream and democratizes structure while relieving game from the logic of banality. From the smallest pun to the largest parodic pattern, comedy asserts its power, not only to amuse or even to surprise us, but far more to multiply meanings, to compound complexities. In this book, comedy is the tuning fork of language, vibrating in a vacuum, forever.

BRIEF COUNTERPOINT

Vacuum. Exactly!

Some would call the infinite vibrations of comedy nihilism. The parody of a parody of a parody that was once comedy. Eternity as absurd recurrence. No evaluation, no value. Is that what "The Gracehoper . . . always jigging ajog, hoppy on akkant of his joyicity" (414.22) has done to the novel?

Still, what major postmodern fiction is conceived but in the comic mode? And who are its ancestors but Joyce and Kafka? Unless it be that obscure man, Raymond Roussel?

PERSPECTIVE IV: STRUCTURE

What can I possibly add to this subject, except perhaps to suggest that all good structuralists go to *Finnegans Wake* on their way to heaven, and that is perhaps why they are so long in reaching their destination?

We know that the novel is both structurally over-determined and semantically under-defined. Its structural principles include numbers, symbols, leitmotifs, collages, montages, mythic patterns, simulated dreams, mystic correspondences, musical ratios, multiple and receding perspectives, game theories, parodies, puns, alliterations, and much else in the lexicon of classical rhetoric. Yet *Finnegans Wake* is not only supremely aware of itself as structure; it is also aware of the more obscure need to de-structure itself. "Samuel Beckett has remarked that to Joyce reality was a paradigm, an illustration of a possibly unstatable rule. Yet perhaps the rule can be surmised," Ellmann says. "It is not a perception of order or of love; more humble than either of these, it is the perception of *coincidence* [italics mine]."

Now coincidence as a structural principle means both identity and accident, recurrence and divergence. Coincidence implies the frightening disorder that every fanatic order itself implies. Four legs of a horse, four seasons, four evangelists. Is this the coincidence of secret design or of dementia in reality? To the very end, Joyce seems to have qualified his emergent vision of correspondences by his ineluctable irony. The more mystical he became—or is it merely superstitious?—the more ruthless his self-parody. His great Dedalian labor includes a deep instinct of unmaking.

Thus, on the one hand, *Finnegans Wake* acknowledges the totality of Joyce's artifice and effort. The ending of Book IV, for instance, may be read to include the endings of all his other works; and various passages of the *Wake* recapitulate the design of the whole novel. But the structure of the novel also reflects upon itself, and in so doing heightens its fictitiousness. The shady character of Shem the Penman, the pervasive motif of the Letter, the reflexive references to Joyce, the wry comments on the manuscript of the novel itself, its progress and reception—"Your exagmination round his factification for incamination of a warping process" (496.36)—all these are instances of artifice recognizing its own artificiality. Thus, on the other hand, *Finnegans Wake* accepts the gratuitousness of every creative act. Indeed, as we shall see, Joyce identified creation with original sin, the most necessary and gratuitous of all acts.

COUNTERPOINT

Shem the Penman, "Sniffer of carrion, premature gravedigger, seeker of the nest of evil in the bosom of a good word" (189.28), Shem, Cain, Satan, Nick and Glugg, Ishmael, Set, Taff and Mutt, Iago, Romeo, Bottom and Puck, Stephen Dedalus, James Joyce, "still today insufficiently malestimated notesnatcher" (125.21), "nay, condemned fool, anarch, egoarch, hiresiarch, you have reared your disunited kingdom on the vacuum of your most intensely doubtful soul" (188.15).

Ah, we say, here is a Portrait of the Artist as Nasty Man. But this artist, Shem Joyce, creates peculiarly postmodern forms and here is why:

a. Parodic Reflexiveness. *The novel that parodies and reflects upon its own structure is not new.* Gide's Les Faux-Monnayeurs

(1925) and Gombrowicz' Ferdydurke (1937), for instance, antecede the Wake in this, as does Tristram Shandy (1760–1767). But the genre, with its multiple, fractured, and ambiguous perspectives, becomes current only after the war in such diverse works as Nabokov's Pale Fire, Cortazar's Hopscotch, Borges' Ficciones, Genet's Journal d'un voleur, Beckett's How It Is, and Barth's Lost in the Fun House.

b. The Re-creation of Reality. *The conventional ideas of time, place, character, plot are shattered; reality is re-created. In modernist literature this is sometimes achieved by a quasi-cubist breakdown of surfaces, as in the works of Gertrude Stein or Alfred Döblin; at other times it is achieved by dissolving surfaces, absorbing them into an interior language, as in the works of Proust or Faulkner. The first method appears quasi-objective, the second quasi-subjective; yet both remake reality in words. Joyce masters both these methods. In that sense,* Finnegans Wake *clears the way for both "neo-realist" and "surrealist" fictions—for Robbe-Grillet's* La Jalousie *and Butor's* Mobile *on the one hand, and Hawkes's* The Cannibal *and Wurlitzer's* Nog *on the other. In either case, the re-creation of reality requires us to abandon the distinction between objective and subjective categories within the pervasive fantasy of the work. Fact and fiction acquire the same aspect. This, too, is postmodern: Capote's "non-fiction novel,"* In Cold Blood; *Styron's "meditation on history,"* The Confessions of Nat Turner; *Mailer's "history as a novel, the novel as history,"* Armies of the Night; *even the New Journalism in America—all these perceive, however partially, that from a certain vantage, fact and fiction must blur. The enormous volume of the World is matched by even greater expansions of the Self until reality becomes a declaration of the mind.*

c. Nonlinear Form. *Circular, simultaneous, coincident—a mesh or mosaic or montage or Moebius time strip of motifs—that, too, is* Finnegans Wake. *We think of myth, music, the cabala, and electrical systems as prototypes of the nonlinear structure of the book, creating a perception that exists outside of conventional time and space. It is not only that time is spatialized as Joseph Frank has argued about the modern novel; in this work both time and space are fantasticated. By rejecting linear or discursive logic, by simulating dream, the* Wake *maintains itself in the "pressant" time and unlimited space of mind. Speaking of Marc Saporta's so-called "shuffle novel,"* Composition No. 1, *Sharon Spencer makes this pertinent point: "Saporta's narrative procedure takes from the dream a rationale for dissolving the conventional distinctions between memory (the past), desire (implying the future), and fantasy (suggesting present being) and for substituting a timeless and preeminently visual mode of organization." Though it appears idiosyncratic, Saporta's work shares with most postmodern fiction the assumption of nonlinear form, which is always visual and inevitably auditory but, above all, seeks to engage the mind directly.*

d. The Problematics of the Book. *Technologies have altered the nature of the book. From Marshall McLuhan to Michel Butor, writers have reflected upon this question; and in* The Stoic Comedians, *Kenner has specifically noted the uses that Joyce made of movable type. It is plain for everyone to see:* Finnegans Wake *employs footnotes, marginalia, lists, sketches, and a variety of types, and it defies sequential reading from cover to cover. More than other works, it is a mixed medium, both discontinuous and whole, visual and auditory, poetic and narrative. Some features of its format may recall the figures of Döblin's* Alexanderplatz Berlin, *the captions of Dos Passos'* U.S.A., *the blanks of Mallarmé's* Un Coup de dés—*may even recall* Gargantua et Pantagruel *or* The Book of Kells. *The same typographic features preview the experiments of John Cage, Ronald Sukenick, Donald Barthelme, Raymond Federman, and Eugene Wildman, to mention only some American postmodernists. But typography is not the real issue; the old concept of the book is at stake. "Throughout* Finnegans Wake," *McLuhan says, "Joyce plays some of his major variation on this theme of 'abcedmindedness'. . . . His 'verbivocovisual' presentation of an 'all nights newsery reel' is the first dramatization of the very media of communication as both form and vehicle of the flux of human cultures." One cannot help but wonder: what will the next verbisensual process of communication in our culture be?*

PERSPECTIVE V: EROTICISM

The eroticism of *Finnegans Wake* is inclusive as its life, varied as its language; yet it remains peculiarly Joycean. Margaret Solomon perceives sex as "Joyce's cosmic joke": "Taking upon himself the role of a God engrossed in sex—and using all the religious myths and symbols of creation to perpetuate his joke—was one way of using his jesuitical training in an act of defiance. . . ." But the *Wake* also goes beyond defiance, and the permutations of sex in it are, unlike Beckett's, both sacred and satiric.

The novel offers a non-Euclidean geometry of sex, as Ms. Solomon shows. People stand for genitals, and diagrams stand for people. Creativity is associated with both waste and generation. There are many entries and exits in nature, and many sensuous sides to every question. As above, so below; as in the beginning, so in the end. But as Fritz Senn notes: "The ups and downs and ins and outs are as erotic as they are political" in Joyce's night-book. The book contains everything Eros and Ellis and Kraft-Ebbing ever dreamed: romantic love, narcissism, coprophilia, incest, sodomy, onanism, lesbianism, voyeurism, exhibitionism, sado-masochism, impotence, every so-called perversion—not to mention the *osculum ad anum diaboli* of the Black Mass—as well as the fruitful love of HCE and ALP: "The galleonman jovial on his bucky brown nightmare. Bigrob dignagging his lylyputtana. One to one bore one!" (583.08).

That is the mystery of love in the novel: the one coming from the many, the many becoming one again. The final point is not perversion but at-one-ment. Thus the composite sexuality of various characters, their male and female "bisectualism," which permits even Mohammed, Shakespeare, and Napoleon to invert their sex. Thus, too, the composite unity of the Earwicker family, which identifies father with sons, mother with daughter, and all with their incestuous counterparts. The sexual fall of Humpty Dumpty signals the eternal metamorphosis of word and flesh, seeking wholeness. Yet Darcy O'Brien says that affection and sensuality are rarely united in Joyce's life or work. Can it be so because final unity is always and wholly impersonal?

COUNTERPOINT

Eroticism in the postmodern age—there are plenty of dirty books now, dirty movies and dirty pictures—imagine Judge Woolsey at a screening of "Deep Throat."

But let us do our age justice.

Consider Norman O. Brown and Norman Mailer—Esalen Institute and Kinsey Institute—Grove Press and Oympia Press— Women's Lib and Gay Liberation—the Pill, Playboy, Penthouse, Portnoy, Pornotopia, and Pornopolitics—all express the dim desire to connect—express the desire and its failure—orgasm as program and sex as solipsism or ideology—yet a new erotic will persists in seeking

larger configurations of itself—the death of the family (David Cooper)
and the search for androgyny (Carolyn Heilbrun)—a new tribalism,
a new polymorphousness and perversity—isn't Finnegans Wake
relevant?

Certainly, but with a difference—it, too, affirms larger configura-
tions of love—a love, however, closer to myth and mutability than
to will and ideology—a love closer still to language—sex as the
language of fantasy—"Psing a Psalm of psexpeans, apocryphul of
rhyme" (242.30)—the sex speech of postmodern fiction?

PERSPECTIVE VI: THE LANGUAGE OF BABEL

"Although it uses the syntax of other languages," Strother Purdy
says of *Finnegans Wake*, "it cannot be considered to be written in
. . . the speech of any group." One wonders: Did Joyce seek to recover the unity of human speech before God said, looking down on
the Tower of Babel: "Go to, let us go down, and there confound their
language, that they may not understand one another's speech"? Frank
Budgen remembers that Joyce once claimed to have discovered the
secret of Babel; but Budgen never asked and we shall never know.

We can guess. Joyce senses that if reality can be identified with
language, language can be identified with itself. This is not to deny
his decreative fury in the *Wake*, his will to silence natural speech, tear
asunder the mother's tongue. But Joyce's fury seeks "words" that can
become im-mediately pure meaning. Harrowing 29 (?) of the world's
languages, he also creates a metalanguage from the chaos of the
world's phonemes, fusing the Viconian modes of hieroglyph, metaphor,
and abstraction.

Joyce, we know, also employs puns, stutters, riddles, seemingly
to arrest the mind in discontinuities. But his puns become metonymies;
the stutters stress recurrence; and even riddles conceal a unity at the
incestuous heart of the universe. However much he owed to the
Jabberwocky of Lewis Carroll, Joyce's own language is less often
analytic than synthetic. His "sentence" is a word in which syntax
gives way to phonemic cluster. From the clear sentences of the earli-
est drafts to the packed, layered interpolations of the last, the process
of Joyce's composition reveals a vast effort of syncretism in which all
the elements of *Finnegans Wake* take part. When Biddy the Hen
pecked out the Letter from the midden heap of time, she may have

discovered the original language of Babel on a soiled palimpsest. "Lead, kindly fowl!" (112.09).

COUNTERPOINT

There is another way of putting it. Finnegans Wake *is "a kind of Logos of the Einsteinian vision of the universe," William Troy wrote in the review which Joyce liked best. But the novel is also "associated with scriptures and sacred books, and treats life in terms of the fall and awakening of the human soul and the creation and apocalypse of nature," Northrop Frye has said. Can we then conclude that in the language of this work the old gnostic and the new technological dream meet, the dream of unifying mind and nature, science and myth, into a single truth—beyond matter?*

I cannot answer. But I am aware that the postmodern endeavor in literature acknowledges that words have severed themselves from things, that language now can only refer to language. And what book, or rather what language, calls attention to itself as language, as ineluctably verbal and quite finally so, more than Finnegans Wake? *John Fletcher understands the influence of Joyce even on the most secretive stylist: "What Beckett really learnt from Joyce was the importance of words and how to make them perform in exercises irrelevant to their superficial meaning but faithful to their essence. . . ."*

The word has become essence indeed, essence or energy, subject to continuous change, yet indestructible and compact like that single book in Borges' "The Library of Babel" which contains all books, past, present, and future, in its infinitesimally thin pages.

PERSPECTIVE VII: TOWARD A UNIVERSAL CONSCIOUSNESS

As I draw to a close, my theme becomes more obvious: *Finnegans Wake* aspires to the condition of a universal consciousness. Consider its design.

Item: Vico says: "Individuality is the concretion of universality, and every individual action is at the same time superindividual"; so it is for Joyce, for whom no character is bound by this time or that place.

Item: Characters are subject to a constant process of recurrence, metempsychosis, and superimposition; and opposites—Shem and Shaun, HCE and ALP—become the other.

Item: The actual and the possible, the historical and the fabulous, have equal validity in eternity; in this gnostic view, Joyce follows Bruno; fact and fiction fuse.

Item: In a world of simultaneity, cause and effect coincide; eternity and the instant merge in the Perpetual Now, as in mystic doctrines; sequence becomes synchronicity.

Item: Joyce chose the night world; as death is the great equalizer so is sister sleep; and in our dreams we exchange all the symbols of the race, without miserliness or shame.

Item: Whoever the Dreamer or Narrator may be, he is All; yet Bernard Benstock is also right: "On the creative level it is Joyce himself giving form to what he has experienced and learned and understood (in the same way in which the Demiurge, creating the universe, dreams away its cycles of evolution)."

Item: The creative process, like the Holy Ghost, invades and unifies all media; television and telepathy, the famous Letter and spirit writing, film and shadows in Plato's cave, copulation and language, become one.

Item: The book wants to include everything; it is not an encyclopedia but a true universe; and through its correspondences of microcosm with macrocosm, it wants to become *the* universe.

The strategies of unification in the novel are as numerous as they have grown familiar. Yet I think many of us have allowed Joyce's demon, called Parody, to obscure this possibility: that the language of *Finnegans Wake* strains toward a gnostic truth. There is a sense in which the totality of the book, its effort toward a universal consciousness, fails to parody or subvert itself, fails to ironicize itself.

James S. Atherton: "Joyce does not deny the existence of sensible material objects. . . . But Berkeley's view of Laws of Nature which he describes in *Siris* as being: 'applied and determined by an Infinite Mind in the macrocosm of universe, with unlimited power and according to stated rules—as it is in the microcosm with limited power and skill by the human mind,' seems to me to be a possible source for the entire structure of the *Wake*."

William Troy: "Humanity is impressive not in its actuality but in its immanence. And this becomes something comparable to the conception of the Divine Idea of the medieval theologians —that which is capable of taking on matter but is itself infinite in time and space."

COUNTERPOINT

"Be that as it may, but for that light phantastic of his gnose's glow as it slid lucifericiously within an inch of its page . . ." (182.04), the postmodern writer might have been like others who have preceded him.

There is a new gnosticism taking hold of our age, a new insistence of Mind to apprehend reality im-mediately and gather more and more mind in itself, a new suspicion of matter, of culture, and even of language insofar as it derives not from the pure logos *but from historical circumstance.*

Much of this new gnosticism comes from technology. Buckminster Fuller speaks of "ephemeralization," whereby energy can be transferred with less and less mediation; Norbert Wiener suggests that man may some day "travel" by telegraph; Marshall McLuhan predicts that electric technology may "by-pass languages in favor of a general cosmic consciousness"; Paolo Soleri calls his new book The Bridge between Matter and Spirit Is Matter Becoming Spirit; *and Dr. José Delgado of the Yale Medical School states: "We are now talking to the brain without the participation of the senses. This is pure and direct communication—I call it nonesensory communication."*

Technology tends toward the direct action of mind on mind, tends toward new kinds of telepathy, telekinesis, and teleportation. Its noetic process, in fact, is similar to Teilhard de Chardin's threefold process—the "vitalization of Matter," the "hominization of Life," and the "planetization of Mankind"—ingathered in the "Noosphere." Thus a physicist, Gerald Feinberg, proposes universal consciousness as a rational goal for mankind in his aptly titled work The Prometheus Project.

*But the germ of the new gnosticism also invades the word-flesh
of literature. It is not only William Burroughs who sees the word as a
"virus" attacking our damaged "central nervous system," preventing
us from enjoying "non-body experience." Less extreme in their
utterances, perhaps, other postmodern authors, both of science and
unscientific fiction, want to dissolve the given world, absorb its
intractable and conditioned elements, into a vision, dream, or afflatus
that may render even language redundant. Whether they are
minimalists like Beckett and Borges or maximalists like Nabokov and
Pynchon, one feels that they strain toward a region of articulate
silence, of intelligent noise, fantasy-filled. This region, which I have
too often attempted to explore, rings, as Susan Sontag says, with "an
energetic secular blasphemy, the wish to attain the unfettered,
unselective, total consciousness of 'God.'"*

Is that not the cry of Finnegans Wake?

POSTAMBLE

"Traduced into jinglish janglage" (275.n6), *Finnegans Wake*, I
repeat, stands as a monstrous prophecy of our postmodernity. In so
many particular ways this seems to me so. But is that prophecy not
ultimately hollow? The query leads to others, and that may be the
way to end.

All my questions about Joyce, all my qualms really, seem to revert
to his peculiar sense of Creation—I mean the creation of life, of people and stars and flowers. God created the world, and that, Joyce believed, was the original sin; for the creative act is always crooked. This
flaw is in all generation, in sex as well as artifice. Thus Joyce could
never see sex without the hidden taint and excitement of error. And
suddenly I find myself wondering: did the lapsarian irony of this
sensualist sometimes turn into final despair and thus turn into a kind
of malice? In fact, how much malice lies in the mocking multiplicity
of *Finnegans Wake*, and how much delight in the fullness of being?
Adaline Glasheen refers to the "good-tempered nihilism" of the novel.
Does the epithet also apply to the Joyce who wrote: "And from time
to time I lie back and listen to my hair growing white . . ."?

Above all, why could Joyce never leave Dublin behind? Never,
never, never, never, never. Whence this obsessive Imagination of
Repetition? "mememormee," "mememormee" is the wail on the last
page of "Finn, again!" Did Joyce really ever conceive a difference be-

tween birth and rebirth, occurrence and recurrence? And is not creation flawed precisely insofar as memory hovers over our copulation and lies in wait for the child as its *given* name?

These questions are perhaps too personal, and may seem too harshly put. Criticism, I know, has its own brand of malice, which I am not eager to display. Nor do I wish to disparage Joyce, who scarcely needs to be praised as a great novelist, among the very greatest to this day. The pilgrimages we all make to these symposia—Joyceans, crypto-Joyceans, meta-Joyceans, and para-Joyceans like myself—are often made in search of learning, sodality, and romance. Still, are they not all begun and concluded in his name?

Yet having emphasized the prophetic sense of Joyce's master riddle, part of me cries (yes, it is the cry of some exorbitant hope akin to pride): Human destiny may be larger than this vast, retrograde, and reversible riddle implies.

Movingly, Hélène Cixous writes: "After Bloom, the deluge, but Joyce had already prepared *Finnegans Wake* as an ark to contain all human myths and types; the world, in its blind lust to seek its own destruction, could wipe itself out, for *Finnegans Wake* had saved its symbols, its notations, and its cultural patterns."

Is this enough for the largest effort of the imagination in our time? Unabashedly, I would ask not only to save the heavy ark, nor only to seek the rainbow sign in the sky, but even to become the very matter of which all rainbows are made. Or perhaps more: NEW LIGHT. . . .

FICTION AND FUTURE:
An Extravaganza for Voice and Tape

I. BEGINNING NOW

We can begin anywhere. Man is a generalist. Buckminster Fuller says: "Nothing seems to be more prominent about human life than its wanting to understand all and put everything together. . . . Man is going to be displaced altogether as a specialist by the computer . . . *automation* displaces *automaton*."

A generalist may find in graffiti a start. I saw a sentence on a crumbling wall the other day: "We have met the enemy and he is us. Pogo." The handwriting on the wall reminds me of Marx. History repeats itself, according to Marx, the first time as tragedy and the next time as farce.

I will come to my topic, contemporary fiction, by and by. I am at my topic, on various levels, now.

II. SCENE: FLASHBACK AND FORWARD [Tape]

A desert road, the sky still and green, a bearded man in the pride of life. Though he is not given to deep knowledge of his acts, he senses the mystery now. Suddenly she is there before him, the Sphinx, monstrous, hungry, bored, managing still a metaphysical leer. She asks the usual question and he answers: "Man!"

Our hero knows how to answer! He has killed an older man at the cross-roads and the strength of murder still stirs in his heart. But his strength falls outwards, outwards; the ordeal remains ahead. Oedipus, King of Thebes, will blind himself and lick the blood in his beard to see what blind Tiresias already knows.

They say that the story of Oedipus is a myth that we dream time and time again. A famous version of the story comes down to us as tragedy, and repeats itself every day as grim farce. The Sphinx endures in stone under Egyptian stars; she no longer needs to waylay or ask.

"We have met the enemy and he is us." But this is also the predicament of gods. Must we then endlessly dream the past?

III.   DREAM, ECOLOGY, AND THE STARS

The dream of Oedipus strikes close to home. In Greek, the study of homes is called ecology. Nowadays, we define ecology as the study of living things in relation to their environment.

But what is the environment of man, that quiddity of life in search of itself? Is it the entire universe, or the earth, or his own consciousness murmuring in the dark? The language of human dreams may vex the farthest star.

This much we know: desire shapes our fictions and our future, and dreams become fact. We create and procreate; and somehow transcend both.

Glimmers of that transcendence light the mind. Perhaps the imagination is the true teleological organ in our evolution, directing all change. Hence the larger interest of fiction and future: our life as it can be, our life now and to come.

I am at my topic now.

IV.   THE LARGE PLACE   [Tape]

We live as strangers in a large place where nothing—no, not even the solitary neutrino—stands apart. Light and gravity, twins of desire, bind the cosmos to our eye and foot. Here is proof:

a.   Some think that the universe breathes, expanding to the limit of gravity and contracting again, forever; some think it began with time in a great bang, never to repeat itself again; and others say that it moves outward into infinity, beyond the speed of light, fed at the center with continuous creation. The dimensions of the universe are five: three in space and one each of time and mass. What are the dimensions of mind?

b.   Astronomers believe that as many galaxies swirl outside our own, the Milky Way, as stars shine within our "island universe." The Milky Way, a mere 100,000 light years across, contains red giants, white dwarfs, blue stars a million times brighter than the sun; and when a supernova explodes, in its unmentionable spaces, it may turn our noon into night. The solar system is but a mote in the cosmic plasm.

Anecdotal

When Charles Messier scanned the skies from his tower in the Hotel de Cluny, looking for comets, he noted 103 cloudy lights that obstructed his sight. He recorded them by numbers, M1, M2, M3 . . . , to avoid them in his search. The clouds proved galaxies beyond the Milky Way, and our neighbor, Andromeda, came to be known as M31.

Anecdotal Ends

c.   Our sun may be no older than five billion years. In five billion years again, the process of fusion at its center—where the temperature is now 25 million °F—will quicken. The sun will swell into a red giant and consume the earth. Then, in another billion years, the sun will begin to shrink, radiating sluggishly an infrared light. Eventually, it will turn cold and black.

A Note on the Chandrasekhar Limit

A static mass 1.4 times that of the sun would, in contracting, develop a gravitational force so great as to vanish, creating a "black hole" in space.

Pulsars come close to this. When a supernova collapses, it may leave behind a neutron star, fifteen miles in diameter, weighing ten billion tons per cubic inch. But this body spins fast, dissipating its gravitational energy in pulses.

Conceivably, then, a super supernova might collapse into a small, quiet ball, heavier than a quintillion suns. Such an object would contract till it vanished from its place in the universe and reappeared elsewhere. In the language of astrophysics, this star would have "encountered a singularity."

Note Ends

d.   Back into the solar system, where nine planets, thirty-two satellites, and countless asteroids circle about, Halley's Comet trails fifty million miles of dust and light. Sighted on the eve of the Norman Conquest, and at regular intervals since then, it will approach the earth in 1986. Shall we decide for life, and arrange to see it again?

e.   Meanwhile, the earth, racing in its orbit, plunges every day into cosmic chaff. It adds two million tons to its mass as it completes a revolution around the sun. Unknowingly, we plough the dust of stars, blown around us by the wind, and drink the universe in a glass of rain.

V. MAPS IN THE MIND

We live in a large place. But we also need maps of "reality" to find our way through the mind. Maps and miracles.

A Memory

As a schoolboy, I used to trace the map of Africa until I learned to draw it with colors, brown, and green, and blue. Though no one had seen the entire African continent, there were maps of it in all the books.

Many years after, they sent a man in space. Imagine, then, my surprise when the first man who saw the entire continent of Africa brought back a photograph identical with the maps I used to trace and draw. Maps are miracles.

Memory Ends

A map on contemporary fiction, however, is another matter; the terrain changes every day. The closer we approach the moment, the harder it is to discern any shape, and even the colors begin to pale. Suddenly, we are in the absolute present: blank. As we move still forward, we begin to fill the map again with fictive shapes which prove our future.

Question: How do we draw Atlantis before Atlantis breaks through the sea? Draw me.

VI. CATEGORIES, CATEGORIES: OLD

We use certain bland categories to describe twentieth-century fiction—the Genteel Tradition, Naturalism, Symbolism—and also invoke the name of each decade—the Twenties, the Thirties, the Forties. For certain obstinate ladies who refuse the spirit of the decades—Ellen Glascow, Sarah Orne Jewett, Willa Cather—we devise a regional label.

A regional label is among the first to adhere to the postwar novel. Here are four categories of fiction since 1945:

a. The Southern Novel. It emerged during the war years as a distinct region of sensibility, detaching itself slowly from Faulkner's Yoknapatawpha County. Eudora Welty and Robert Penn Warren helped to firm its outline.

Names: Carson McCullers, Flannery O'Connor, the early Styron or Capote, William Goyen, Peter Taylor, Shirley Ann Grau, Walker Percy, Reynolds Price, others.

b. The Jewish Novel. Northern rather than Southern, urban rather than rural, more liberal than traditionalist in its sympathies, Jewish fiction harked back to Nathanael West, Henry Roth, and Daniel Fuchs, though its main impact began in the late forties.

Names: Saul Bellow, Bernard Malamud, J. D. Salinger, Leslie Fiedler, Herbert Gold, Bruce Jay Friedman, Edward Lewis Wallant, Stanley Elkin, others.

c. The Negro Novel (not yet Black). It began South and ended North; its geographical migration became a quest for identity. Its father, Richard Wright, is now both honored and repudiated.

Names: Ralph Ellison, James Baldwin, John A. Williams, William Melvin Kelley, Paule Marshall, others.

d. The Beat Novel. Committed to vision and apostasy, the Beats did not name a region their own; they lived subterraneanly or on the road. Like their predecessor, Henry Miller, they braved sentimentality and shared his wonder, lust, and spontaneity.

Names: Jack Kerouac, Lawrence Ferlinghetti, Gregory Corso, John Clellon Holmes, others.

How quaint these categories now seem, like a Ptolemaic map illustrated with dragons, sea serpents, and the puffy face of wind! By the late fifties many names had begun to recede or else had moved into new countries. Critics looked for other terms—"black humor," "Camp," "the nonfiction novel," "the literature of silence," "the new mutants"—to describe the changing scene. Certainly, some exciting novelists of the last two decades—Mailer, Barth, Vonnegut, Nabokov, Burroughs, Purdy, Hawkes, Pynchon, Barthelme—evade the old categories.

VII. SOME QUERIES ON CURRENT FICTION

There are still many gifted Southern writers. Why then, has the Southern novel ceased to hold a charmed place? The decline of formalist criticism may be a factor; Brooks, Warren, Ransom, and Tate, great formalists, are Southerners. The Civil Rights movement and the Black Power movement have also qualified the myth of the South. Or is it simply that the enormous present—poverty, pollution, rebellion, Vietnam—deflects our attention from the language of the past?

* * *

Both Southern and Jewish fiction depend upon the telling of tales. A story implies a society, a community of listeners. "Once upon a time": we say that in a circle. This affirms a recoverable past. In the Jewish novel, particularly, the story may bear a sacramental message as in Hassidic narratives. It is evidence of *emunah*, the holy persistence of Israel—see S. Y. Agnon's *The Bridal Canopy*, a patchwork of somber and bright tales. But the story may also bite the bitter rind of modernity—see Elie Wiesel's *A Beggar in Jerusalem*, which bears transcendent witness to past inhumanity and mortal interdebtedness beyond death, waiting, waiting always, testifying to the end.

* * *

What, then, is a story? Scheherezade may have known the answer: so long as she can tell a tale, she lives. A story races against death, and in ending reminds us of the End. Hemingway states that all true stories must terminate in death. Beckett agrees: his unnamable heroes drone endlessly, seeking release from the stories thy are condemned to tell, seeking the final stillness. When Nabokov cries, Speak Memory! he cries against the onrushing night. But a wild-eyed beggar in Wiesel's novel makes the best point of all: "Remember, child, remember that the day someone tells you your life, you will not have much longer to live." Perhaps stories always have two authors: Voice and Silence, the Ego and its Death.

* * *

Suppose that Western man learns to unfear egoistic death. Like Orpheus, he may sing, and singing become part of nature, bird and tree, stone and cloud. Singing Orpheus releases himself into the universe. With his electric lyre, can he wed technology to mythology? Can he define for us a new ecology? No more stories, then, no selections and arrangements of our lives; everything will be there at once, wired to eternity. Is this why some anti-novelists declare their distrust of stories? I think that I may read into them too much.

* * *

We are not wired to eternity yet. We are in an age of transition. We are always in an age of transition but some transitions are more disjunctive than others. My angry students seldom read novels now. They read Malcolm X, Fanon, Cleaver, Mao, Debray, Marcuse, Goodman, McLuhan, Brown, Buber, Fuller, Cage, Watts. They also listen to songs and rock. Has fiction failed the revolutionary imagination of our time? Or must it by its very nature so fail? Is this why Styron's *The Confessions of Nat Turner* finally grates? But when Bob Dylan sings "Subterranean Homesick Blues," he gives to the Weathermen their name. There may be more in *The Whole Earth Catalog* to frame a new consciousness than the usual art novel contains.

* * *

What about the new Black Novel? How revolutionary is it? Here the paradoxes thicken. William Demby's remarkable work *The Catacombs* breaks down Western civilization—Pirandello, Picasso, Stein, Heisenberg, McLuhan, Chardin, Kennedy, Khrushchev, DeGaulle, the Pope—and puts it back again together in pure forms of the mind. Less subtle, Cecil Brown's *The Life and Loves of Mr. Jiveass Nigger* diverts anger and truth into knowing games. Amiri Baraka's (LeRoi Jones) *The System of Dante's Hell*, however, devises a kaleidoscope of violence against Others, against Self, against God, Nature, and Art. Its sounds and images burn the dross of America and purify Jones's own life in it. There is spell, curse, poetry, and exorcism in the novel. Can revolution become poetry? Perhaps the Black Novel has chosen the way of black surrealism. Yet some questions remain: carried to a certain level of complexity or intensity what action does imagination prescribe? What is the color of the brain?

VIII. THE SMALL PLACE   [Tape]

I have spoken of the large place; now for its smaller counterpart, no less prodigal or strange.

a.   Whenever the human brain entered biological evolution, a million or two years ago, attending the club-clutching hand and word-wagging tongue, it is here to stay if we stay. We carry it about as a woman carries her unborn child, in a womb of bone, floating delicately in the cerebrospinal fluid, protected by the *dura mater* and the *pia mater,* with the tough *arachnoid* in between. Two mothers for the human brain, and the third is a spider web.

b.   The brain devours energy. Weighing no more than a fiftieth of the body's weight, it still consumes a fifth of the body's air and blood. Yet this devourer can reverse the entropy of the universe by increasing the order of things; or as Buckminster Fuller would say, by synergetics, the art of "doing more with less." No muscle twitches in the head as ten billion neurons work in their place. When their work is finally done, who knows but that the universe may become pure mind, Teilhard de Chardin's "noösphere."

c.   But the brain is not yet whole or one. Like a divided flower, never exposed to the sun, it grows from an ancient stem that controls both heart and lungs. On each side, cerebellum, thalamus, and limbic system twice grasp the stem. Our muscles, our senses, our rages and fears and loves, stir about in this double fistful of old matter. The great new cortex envelops the whole, gray petals and convolutions, where will, reason, and memory strive to shape all into mind. Left brain, right hand, language and logos; right brain, left hand, violence and nonverbal arts. They do not acknowledge one another. Yet a computer's magnetic tape would need to run several million miles to memorize what a single cortex easily recalls.

d.   Now they tell us of strange foods for the brain. Peyote, belladonna, thornapple, hemp, and henbane can alter our perceptions; psilocybin, from sacred mushrooms, and lycergic acid, from ergot, can alter them more. Molecular biology promises to change man's behavior, intelligence, and memory in drastic ways. Scientists have already cracked the molecular code of RNA. Soon the prediction of J. B. S. Haldane, that our children will come into the world speaking perfect English, may be fulfilled. Or will they speak perfect Russian or perfect Chinese? No one yet knows how to answer the question: "Who decides what happens to whom?"

Anecdotal

"At the University of Michigan, Dr. Bernard W. Agranoff has experimented with a 'memory erasure' drug called puromycin. Its effects on animals were spectacular.

"When asked by a reporter whether the Central Intelligence Agency has an interest in his work, Dr. Agranoff would only smilingly reply, 'I forget.'" David M. Rorvik, Avant-Garde, *March, 1970.*

Anecdotal Ends

e.   But what is the secret mission of the brain? Writing in the early nineteenth century, Sir Charles Sherrington describes the brain as "an enchanted loom where millions of flashing shuttles weave a dissolving pattern, always a meaningful pattern though never an abiding one." The brain creates perpetual patterns with a purpose, and among these are dreams. Neurologists now know that the brain dreams rhythmically. Night after night, with the regularity of universal motions, it gives itself to fictions and prophecies, with rapid eye movements.

IX.   THE MAP OF VANISHING FICTION

More novels are published today than ever before, and the proportion of "good novels" among these may be the highest yet. Still, I offer this possibility: that the novel may be a form undergoing deep mutations. I hope that the result will be something rich and strange.

Here is my Map of Vanishing Fiction:

Imagine two lines meeting at some point in the future. Call the left line the Novel of Silence, or as Barth would say, the Literature of

Exhaustion. Call the right line the Fantastic Novel, or as Vonnegut would want, Science Fiction. The area between these lines is the literary domain, and it is filled with all manner of fictions. Most of these fictions acknowledge the boundaries that enclose them; that is, acknowledge their future.

Here are some recent examples, in the middle ground of fiction:

a. Close to the center, the work of Joyce Carol Oates seems to celebrate darkly the traditional pieties of the novel, and to deny that the genre contemplates its own end. Let us admit that she shows, in her many novels, a certain faith in the shapeliness of experience. But let us also note: her gothic experience includes, above all, the experience of nothingness, *nada,* which her works attempt to exorcise in vain. Moreover, *Expensive People* begins to play with fictional forms, incorporating reviews of itself, discussing the "death of the novel," referring to Fiedler's *Waiting for the End,* etc. In later pieces, "Matter and Energy," and "How I Contemplated the World . . . ," Oates opens up the narrative further; she presents us with fragments of diary and reflection. The notes of a "delinquent" girl for an essay become the story form.

b. Consider next Daniel Stern's novel, *The Suicide Academy.* Superficially, the work treats the confrontation of Black and Jew with insight into their complexities and complicities. But the work attempts more: it attempts, in the author's words, "to create a kind of para-reality; to give the imagination the concreteness and density of palpable truth while endowing it with as much strangeness and metaphoric reach as it will bear. In fact, just a little more than it can bear! Each element balances its opposite: an institution where you go when you wish to decide on committing suicide or not . . . this is balanced by a man's re-experienced love for his ex-wife."

c. In *Steps,* Jerzy Kosinski creates the cunning and cruel identity of Self from the discontinuum of experience. The Self slips, changes, contracts, leaving before us terrible lacunae and blank spaces. "Given the reader's experiences . . . ," Kosinski says in his notes on the novel, "the reader may perceive the work in a form of his own devising, automatically filling in its intentionally loose construction with his own formulated experiences and fantasies. . . . At the end of every consecutive incident *Steps* allows the reader to break his journey—or to continue reading. In the fissure separating these possibilities the struggle between the book (the predator) and the reader (the victim) takes place."

Now, as we move farther from the center, the double tendency implicit in these works begins to emerge: self-parody or play, irreality or surreality, autodestruction or transcendence pull the novel toward its boundaries. At one boundary, that of Silence or Exhaustion, the novel moves toward abolition of its form. At the other, of Fantasy or Science Fiction, it moves beyond itself into vision. But these are limits, and before we reach them, we need to survey our domain more. Consider, then, these works (left of center) tending toward the Silence of old forms:

a. Stanley Berne and Arlene Zekowski, husband and wife, have written between them some dozen works. They call their method "Neo-Narrative." They believe that the sentence today is dead because it is founded on a dead language, Latin. In *Seasons of the Mind*, Zekowski says: "Precisely just with words, a new field of perception must be created where the old elements will undergo something akin to a chemical and physical metamorphosis in order for new compounds and new substances to enter literature and vivify and extend its entire frame of reference." And in *The Unconscious Victorious*, Berne claims: "We may be coming to the end of the era for books, but not, be it noted, to the end of the need for the literary experience, for that will live on by way of other media." Both seek to recover, in a new grammar of images, the arcane continuity of life, without plot, character, or common syntax.

b. The title of Ronald Sukenick's work, *The Death of the Novel and Other Stories*, speaks jauntily for itself. Sukenick breaks up the printed page in aphorisms, news captions, simultaneous narratives, parallel columns, dadaist collages, run-on sentences held together by zany, angry humor. He quotes Beckett and repeats the refrain: "I can't go on / Go on." He quotes Wallace Stevens: "A violent order is disorder." He notes: "The didactic job of the modern novel is to teach people to invent themselves and their world—Robbe-Grillet." He simulates a tape recorder, a candid camera, an advanced honors seminar on "The Death of the Novel." He ends a section called "Momentum" by saying: "I'm happy, folks, and I wish you luck. I disappear around the bend." He mentions Spock, Coffin, the students of Columbia and the Sorbonne, shows us the absurd in home and street. Thus farce and slapstick blend with the obdurate and banal facts of our day in improvisations on an old question: how can the imagination take power again, pervade our lives, and alter the quality of existence?

c. Earl M. Rauch calls his book *Dirty Pictures from the Prom*. It contains pointless epigraphs, blank and crossed-out pages, a few "obscene" drawings, chapters sketched only in outline, a running dialogue between Author and Editor at the end of each chapter, as commentary on the main narrative. Throughout the novel, quotations also appear from a certain work, *Dialogue with an Unkown Black-Veiled Madame on the Coach Ride to Tours* by Creynaldo. Creynaldo is the brother of Barnaby, the narrator; Creynaldo dies at the age of seven, and he has some attributes of Christ or of Completeness. This desperate hoax of a book turns out to be a mystic pursuit of time, a quest for original freedom, a search for consciousness, Being. Deadpan, Rauch moves from farce to degradation and sheer terror, exposing that ultimate evil: the disguises of human absence, Nonbeing. Here farce and fiction strain their resources till the reader must either dismiss the work as trivial or else admit its outrage.

A Bibliographical and Reflective Note   [Tape]

Other works in the same genre have appeared in the last few years, and some of them appear more exotic or extreme. Inevitably, when the imagination reaches toward the limit of a certain art form, radical changes in the expectations of the audience take place. See the following works:

Marvin Cohen, *The Self-Devoted Friend*
John Brockman, *By the Late John Brockman*
Andy Warhol, *A*

There are also "concrete novels," "shuffle novels," and "blank novels," a bound sheaf of pages to remind us that silence can also be literal and white.

Carlyle, however, celebrated the virtues of silence through thirty volumes. Why is this a joke? The language of paradox is as old as human consciousness, an integral part of its most complex functions. No animal can think or utter: "I do not exist."

Note Ends

Let us move on to some other works on the right of our imaginary center. Let us move toward Fantasy, though we may never have left it.

a. Richard Brautigan has written several works, poems and novelettes, evoking a simple and marvelous life. *Trout Fishing in America* and *In Watermelon Sugar* seem limpid as a mountain stream flashing metaphors in sunlight. His dislocation of language is subtle, sweet, and funny; we end by floating in another element, released from all our habits. Parody and poetry, nostalgia and satire, nature and human incongruity, death itself, dart between words rounded smooth as pebbles. Here is the outcome of intercourse between a gentle couple in a hot spring: "My sperm came out into the water, unaccustomed to the light, and instantly it became a misty, stringy kind of thing and swirled out like a falling star, and I saw a dead fish come forward and float into my sperm, bending it in the middle. His eyes were like iron." Brautigan hurries from scene to short scene—his "chapters" are sometimes no longer than their headings—as his novels disclose within the reader some enchanted inscape of green leaves, laughter, memories, a vision of the American Garden "with real toads in it."

Digression

The toads in our visionary garden become every day more loathesome. The New York Times: *"Dallas, March 28 (UPI) Larry Joe Knox, 23 years old, has been sentenced to 1001 years in prison—the longest term in Texas history—for raping a young telephone operator. It was the third big prison term handed down in the Dallas–Fort Worth area this month."*

Digression Ends

b. The fantasy of Rudolph Wurlitzer's *Nog* is calmly deranged and nocturnal. This "headventure," as the subtitle calls it, takes us through outer America—a land of Indians, desert rats, acidheads, outcasts—on the silent wings of Nog's madness. Indeterminacy guides both motive and perception: "Delicate moment, when the line draws taut, when the lurching from wall to wall suddenly ends. I will miss the complaining and the whining. . . . Where do these words come from? There's no need for them now. But they dribble on. Nog, of course, can become clearer. Or dropped. Or simply forgotten." This will remind us of Beckett's *Watt*. But Nog, who speaks of himself in the third person—schizoids do that too—is a different breed of solipsist. He subsists on white pills, sharing his life with a couple, Lockett and Meredith, whom he finally destroys. "I don't know if I can remember anyone who is apart from me for very long," he manages to conclude. Nog's consciousness, like the rubber octopus in the novel, is not merely an artifact, nature aberrant; his author succeeds in giving it the hues of our own madness.

c. "Patarealism," a term coined by Ishmael Reed, best describes his novel, *Yellow Back Radio Broke-Down*. The book brings together elements of the tall tale, horse opera, circus, absurd humor, and "Hoo-Doo," a madcap version of African juju adapted to Black fiction. Phrases like "crazy dada nigger," "far-out esoteric bullshit," "the cosmic jester" also suggest the quality of character and action, fancy and wordplay, in this work. As the hero, the Loop Garoo Kid, puts it to another: "What's your beef with me Bo Schmo, what if I write circuses? No one says a novel has to be one thing. It can be anything it wants to be, a vaudeville show, the six o'clock news, the mumblings of wild men saddled by demons." Words spark as anger and anarchy strike in Reed's imagination. Its violence and humor destroy all sham, and would destroy the whole world rather than yield in fantastic freedom.

We are rather more used to this genre of fantasy than to fictions of exhaustion. The novels of Joseph Heller, J. P. Donleavy, Thomas Pynchon, Thomas Berger, William Gass, Donald Barthelme, among others, have conditioned us to desperate burlesque and humor. But in responding to their extravagant ironies, we tend to ignore their hidden visionary qualities, and so convert them into Camp. Bizarre, satirical, and excessive, they still imply a world, in some undiscovered corner of the heart, where love binds the tiger and the lamb, and the child remains father to the man.

Surmise

Recent and remarkable, the works I have cited suggest that fiction moves toward subversion or transcendence of itself, and sometimes moves toward both at once. The way down and the way up are the same. Perhaps only the transfiguration of reality, into something or nothing, matters. Anything can happen. Is the conclusion to fiction Cage?

X. THE VISIONS OF PRACTICAL MEN

Enclosed with my bill for the month of January, 1970, *Telephone News* declares:

"The Age of Aquarius, famous from astrology and popular music, is a wonderful vision of a peaceful and happy world. . . .

"But it takes interpreters and practical men to make visions come true. We in the communications industry are trying to help those dreams along. . . .

"How would you like to have a phone that shops for you, locks your door and controls your stove? We're working on it.

"And how about dialing a computerized library for information—in spoken and printed words, pictures or diagrams—or doing your math problems just by pushing the keys of your Touch-Tone telephone?

"Handling money could be revolutionized too. A phone call to your bank's computer will take care of payments on your regular authorized bills such as rent or utilities. It could also keep track of your balance, and even figure out your income tax.

"To help you stay healthy, your doctor could draw on the entire sum of medical knowledge through his telephone.

"Yes, 1970 and beyond looks pretty exciting."

Fuller: "So I'll say to you that man on earth is now clearly faced with the choice of Utopia or Oblivion."

XI. WHERE BOUNDARIES MEET

In a universe curved positively, a beam of light radiating from a man's eye will travel to the boundaries and return to hit him, many billion years after, in the back of the skull.

But the boundaries of fiction meet within the skull. In my imaginary map, the Novel of Silence and the Fantastic Novel converge on some point in the future, and their convergence helps to draw the future in our midst.

Let me now speak of each limit at some length.

A. *The Novel of Silence and Exhaustion*

For almost two centuries now, a particular kind of literature has made itself by denying the assumptions of art, form, and language. We call the most recent expressions of this spirit anti-literature. But the tradition of silence is really deeper in reach and wider in scope. It may revert to Sterne's *Tristram Shandy* or Sade's *Justine*, include certain Romantic and Symbolist poets, notably Lautréamont and Rimbaud, who drove language berserk, and erupt finally in the modern avant-garde: 'Pataphysics, Dadaism, Futurism, Surrealism, etc.

Anecdotal

Alfred Jarry, 'Pataphysician, went about with a pair of revolvers in his belt. His favorite expression was, "Isn't it beautiful, like literature?" The Dadaists took their cue from him and wrote their manifestoes with bullet holes. As for Marcel Duchamp, alias Marchand du Sel alias Rrose Sélavy, grand master of chess, silence, and art, he consecrated a urinal into art and gave the Mona Lisa a mustache.

Anecdotal Ends

In the novel, particularly, the exhaustion of form and consciousness becomes an explicit theme in a sequence of French works: Gide's *The Counterfeiters,* Sartre's *Nausea,* Beckett's *Watt,* and Robbe-Grillet's *The Labyrinth.* We can say about the authors of these original fictions what John Barth said in his essay "The Literature of Exhaustion," about the Argentinian Jorge Luis Borges: "His artistic victory . . . is that he confronts an intellectual dead end and employs it against itself to accomplish new human work. . . . In homelier terms, it's a matter of every moment throwing out the bath water without for a moment losing the baby."

Barth should know. Like Beckett, Borges, and Burroughs, he has turned "the death of the novel" to enormous advantage, and given us in *The Sot-Weed Factor* and *Giles Goat-Boy* works which, in his own words, "imitate the form of the Novel, by an author who imitates the role of Author." *Lost in the Fun House* goes further than self-parody: it appropriates techniques other than the novel's, and thus offers itself to translation into another medium. The living voice, the printed word, and the magnetic tape constitute a kind of aural montage in the book, a generic conceit. The narrative swallows itself by the tail, as in "Anonymiad," or vanishes in a Chinese box, as in "Menelaiad." These tricks refine an old dream of Barth. Fabulously inventive, Barth finds the phenomenal world odd, gratuitous: "Which snowflake triggers the avalanche?" Reality is merely "a nice place to visit." Beginning with *The Floating Opera,* his heroes emerge as ironists of history and their own flesh, without connection to the earth, yet marvelously free, funny, and lucid in the realm of "ultimacy," which lies beyond fancy. The virtuosity of their author sustains them, lends them inverted vitality. But Barth knows that high wit no longer suffices and ultimacy may literally end in the void. In a piece called "Title," he takes up the predicament of the tale, the teller, and the told: "What is there to say at this late date? Let me think, I'm trying to think. Same old story. Or. Or? Silence." "Title" is an internal argument, with voice and tape and print, assent and skepticism and denial playing against one another, concluding nothing. The last sentence trails in a blank space: "How in the world will it ever

A Digression on Tapes   [Tape]

John Cage, Samuel Beckett, John Barth, playing with tapes and magnetism.

Cage: the tape as a voice other than one's own; as past made present in instant replay, hence simultaneity; as a different parameter of awareness, a new source of sound; as random order when several tapes play together; the sound of pantheism.

Beckett: Krapp's last tape as repetition, time that will not come to a stop; as the first person speaking on and on, forever; as static, noise, decay in communication; the sound of solipsism.

Barth: the tape as an aural mask for the narrator; as voices playing with mirrors, dispelling their identity; as language in its essence, without decaying flesh; the sound of nihilism.

There is also Heinrich Böll. The old man in his story "Doktor Murkes" spends his life splicing the silences on the tapes of others to make his own tape.

Note, however, that the magnetic tape still depends on mechanics: reels, buttons, springs, motors. Only our familiar television, McLuhan says, is all electric, in sympathy with our brains.

B.   The Fantastic Novel and Science Fiction

This genre has an old and diverse history. It may revert to Plato's myth of Atlantis in the *Timaeus* and Lucian of Samosata's voyages to the moon in the *True Histories*. It may draw on More's *Utopia* and all its ghastly sequels: Zamyatin's *We*, Orwell's *Nineteen Eighty-Four*, Huxley's *Brave New World*. It owes something to fantastic voyages and tales: *Sinbad the Sailor, Gulliver's Travels, The Adventures of Baron von Munchausen*. It also enriches itself from the large and disparate body of horror stories, gothic novels, allegorical narratives, and visionary literature. We know that Francis Bacon, Johannes Kepler, Francis Godwin, and Cyrano de Bergerac all wrote, before the nineteenth century, *ur* science fictions. But we agree that Jules Verne and H. G. Wells gave the genre its modern aura and authority. After the second world war, the gates of the technological dream seemed suddenly to open, flooding our unconscious. The creations of Ray Bradbury, Arthur Clarke, Robert Heinlein loom hugely in colors on our screens. The Hugo and Nebula awards become almost as newsworthy as a Pulitzer Prize or National Book Award.

The genre really needs no pedantic definition. Wells thinks that it entails the ingenious use of "scientific patter," and Kingsley Amis notes that "*Idea as hero*" is the basis of science fiction. Bradbury gives an even broader view of fantasy: "To make the extraordinary seem ordinary, and cause the ordinary to seem extraordinary." The serious point to be made about science fiction is this: it offers critiques of the human condition and fashions new myths from the old; and, going further still, it offers radical alternatives to the destiny we assume to be our own. The best of science fiction, then, does not merely display "a mode of romance with a strong inherent tendency to myth," as Northrop Frye says; it brings, rather, intimations of a consciousness that has not yet found its myth. In short, the best of science fiction looms as true prophecy or vision.

A Digression on the New   [Tape]

Prophecy is akin to madness, Cassandra raving, the Pythoness of Apollo in a trance.

Prediction is extrapolation: we simply extend the past and present into the future and project what we already know. Nothing new.

Prophecy *creates* the new. Deranged, the mind creates the future. We sometimes call this shaping derangement of things imagination!

Prophecy is akin to madness and the creative imagination, but in biological terms it is also akin to mutation. Consider nature. The conservative instincts, the codes in the double helix, repeat and repeat the forms of life into eternity. Fanatic conservatism of the genes. But there are also random mutations: suddenly something incomprehensible occurs, something new. Thus certain breakthroughs in evolution: photosynthesis, the vertebrates, the cerebral cortex.

Who says nothing is new under the sun? Who says nothing is new by the light of the moon?

Digression Ends

Among contemporary writers, Kurt Vonnegut stands out as a gruff sentimentalist with a soft spot in his heart for science fiction. One of his characters, Eliot Rosewater, says to practitioners of the genre: "I love you sons of bitches. . . . You're all I read any more. You're the only ones who'll talk about the *really* terrific changes going on, the only ones crazy enough to know that life is a space voyage. . . . You're the only ones with guts enough to *really* care about the future. . . ." Vonnegut himself often wavers between the future and the past, the story in its slickest form and the vision of things to come, the bombings of Dresden and the destiny of the planet Tralfamadore.

Furthermore, some of his science fiction—*Player Piano, Welcome to the Monkey House*—is in the old form of dystopia: an extension of the absurd or destructive tendencies of the present, a scientized homily, satire, or warning. This is understandable; Vonnegut is really a simple moralist, haunted by the reality of death. (The refrain "so it goes, so it goes" follows each mortal event in *Slaughterhouse Five*, like water drops in Chinese torture.) Typically, his own moral confession sounds a bit cute: "And I realize now that the two main themes of my novels were stated by my siblings: 'Here I am cleaning shit off of practically everything' and 'No pain.' "

Still, neither prophylaxis nor anaesthesia constitute all his interests; Vonnegut has another visionary side. In *The Sirens of Titan*, for instance, destiny is not causal or temporal as we usually think; destiny embraces the sum total of love in the universe, the power of the Universal Will to Become. As for the government of Tralfamadore, Salo describes it as "hypnotic anarchy," adding: "Either you understand at once what it is . . . or there is no sense in trying to explain it to you. Skip." The nature of Tralfamadorian fiction proves especially relevant to my theme. A voice describes it in *Slaughterhouse Five*: "Each clump of symbols is a brief, urgent message—describing a situation, a scene. We Tralfamadorians read them all at once, not one after the other. There is no beginning, no middle, no end, no suspense, no moral, no causes, no effects. What we love in our books are the depths of many marvelous moments, seen all at one time."

But time warps, spaceships, and galactic materializations aside, Vonnegut, an earthling like all of us, cannot push his vision past the ironic barrier of the mind. He bestows on his ideal creatures, the Tralfamadorians, the supreme privilege of blowing up the universe. They blow it up, of all things, experimenting with a new fuel for their flying saucers. So much, then, for universal Time and Space, where vision and extinction finally become one.

And so the boundaries of fiction twice meet.

They meet first as our map folds into a headless cone, bringing the lines of Silence and of Fantasy together into a single seam. Thus Barth and Vonnegut exchange hilarious hints of oblivion. Thus also Nabokov, in *Ada*, brings together all our themes, and creates, in *Pale Fire*, a vision of eternity through self-canceling forms. Other writers, as different as Burroughs and Pynchon, multiply their fabulism with naught.

But the boundaries, two sides of the cone, meet again at some future point where the apex hides. There, beyond where Silence and Fantasy exhaust themselves, a new form of art, of consciousness, may lie.

Caveat

Here are works that I failed to name:
  a. Hawkes's The Lime Twig
  b. Malamud's The Fixer
  c. Cohen's The Beautiful Losers
  d. Bellow's Mr. Sammler's Planet
There are many others. Who says the novel is dying?

XII. FOR THE HUMANISTS [Tape]

The important questions before the human race are not literary questions. They are questions of consciousness—reason, dream, love—since consciousness affects the use of our physical means. Humanists have something to say in the matter though most prefer to keep the Humanities in the museum stage.

But even museums change: they lose their walls. Curators and critics of art, Harold Rosenberg shows, turn their eyes on the future, and historians help to make art history rather than wait for that history to be made. Custodians of the word, however, usually have a heavier mien. This sadness is not merely in academe. Compare the Arts and Books sections in a popular magazine: their authors seem to hail from different centuries.

We need not walk like amnesiacs in history to keep the mission of the Humanities alive. John McHale writes: "To invent the future we need, in certain senses, to reinventory the past." The literary past is full of mutability; it guarantees the persistence of no genre or form. Epic, romance, ballad, sermon, pastoral, sonnet have all seen their brightest day. What piety, then, compels us to regard the novel eternal? Is bourgeois society, matrix of the novel, the end of all History?

New media have come into our midst since the printing press—telephone, film, comic strip, television, xerox, computer—and it is still hard to know how these and future media will affect the literary response, will alter the needs of the imagination. The time for large speculation may have caught up with us, may soon leave us far behind.

Scientists know that modern technology does not only create a new reality for mankind; it also permits the coexistence of several realities. Coexistence takes place in a context of universal sentience. Here is McHale again: "This idea of organized human thought now covering the globe as a functional part of the overall ecological system is, to an extent, physically demonstrable in our present global communications network. . . ."

Humanists must enter the sphere of active symbols now surrounding the earth, and bring to it what they know of language and the sovereign imagination. Humanists must enter the future. They must also dream.

XIII. SCIENCE AND PROPHECY, FICTION AND FUTURE

Galileo, staring too long at the sun, turned blind, and the Inquisition trod on his tongue. Seers endure constraints on speech and sight. Nostradamus, also looking heavenward, chose to write his *Centuries* "by abstruse and twisted sentences . . . under a figure cloudy rather than plainly prophetic." Deep in his "ecstatic work, amid prolonged calculation, and engaged in nocturnal studies of sweet odour," Nostradamus still sought a unifying concept for all his shadowy labors. "The reason is too evident," he says in a preface; "the whole is predicted by the afflatus of divinity. . . ."

Someday it may be possible to place both astronomy and astrology within a larger and simpler frame, some vast noetic vision of things, or as Wordsworth put it:

> Characters of the great Apocalypse
> The types and symbols of Eternity.

Meantime, we do well to ponder the words of an eminent savant, Sir James Jeans: "Mind no longer appears as an accidental intruder in the realm of matter. We are beginning to suspect that we ought rather to hail it as the creator and governor of the realm of matter." Perhaps this is where science and prophecy meet: in deep fictions of the mind, still locked in emblems of our sleep.

Our view of human consciousness remains at best limited, and we limit it even more by defining it in individual terms only. Our investigations of the Freudian unconscious draw us, willy-nilly, into psychic realms larger than a single organism, longer than the life span of any man. We begin to mumble about "memory traces," "the oceanic feeling," "the collective unconscious." We even wonder if the unconscious contains the possibilities of future experience, a life waiting to be lived. Is the child, then, really father to the man, and time reversible?

We do not really know.

Anecdotal

Freud charted the mind, its surface and depths. He found his way among its terrors. He also loved to hike in spring and summer. When

*he went out, looking for mushrooms and wild flowers, he always got
lost in the woods.*

Anecdotal Ends

Yet something tells us that dream looks back to myth and forward
to prophecy, sharing with both certain forms and wisdom. There are
also in science certain forms that will dream us onward, and extend
our senses to the limits of the invisible universe. It is no longer enough
for man to rely simply on his common senses. Already he entrusts his
life every day, on land and air and sea, to secret extensions. Where is
the limit of sight or touch?

Man must dream himself onward: he has grown tired of the back
of the primeval cave. Though he may meet at the end of his journey
the same face he left behind him, he must continue his way. And who
is there to say that, at the end, the face to greet him may not be a
transfiguration of his own?

It is always journey time, and new fictions may give man a map
for a small part of the way.

THE NEW GNOSTICISM:
Speculations on an Aspect of the
Postmodern Mind

I. EPIGRAPHS*

Thine own consciousness, shining, void, and in-
separable from the Great Body of Radiance, hath
no birth, nor death, and is the Immutable Light.

The Gospel of Truth is *joy* for those who have received the *grace* of *knowing* from the Father of
Truth. . . . He who knows is a being from above.
If he is called, he hears, he replies, he turns to him
who calls him, in order to come back to him. . . .
He who thus possesses gnosis knows whence he
has come and whither he goes.

The Circumference is Within, Without is formed the
Selfish Center, / And the Circumference still expands going forward to Eternity. . . .

The sublime remark of Euler on his law of arches,
"This will be found contrary to all experience, yet
is true," had already transferred nature into the
mind, and left matter to be an outcast corpse.

The origins of the process of mechanization are
more mystical than we imagine.

The universe begins to look more like a great
thought than like a great machine.

Spiritualized Energy is the flower of Cosmic Energy.
To dominate and canalize the powers of the air and
the sea is all very well. But what is this triumph,
compared with the world-wide mastery of human
thought and love?

* Epigraph references are on last page of this section.

Today computers hold out the promise of a means of instant translation of any code or language into any other code or language. The computer, in short, promises by technology a Pentecostal condition of universal understanding and unity. The next logical step would seem to be, not to translate, but to bypass languages in favor of a general cosmic consciousness. . . .

All scientific generalizations
Are pure metaphysics
All metaphysics are weightless
And physically unlimited.

Because of the millennial nature of the goal of extending consciousness, we can expect that, if we adopt it, it will exert a small but persistent influence on human activities over a very long period of time.

The real world . . . is the world where thoughts are omnipotent, where no distinction is drawn between wish and deed. As in the New Testament. . . .

We are actually born out of light, you might say. I believe light is the maker of all material. Material is spent light.

But what do twelve epigraphs prove?

Surely they do not answer an appeal to authority since few of us now accept the same authorities.

Do they evoke a mood, declare a theme, insinuate a conclusion? Possibly. Yet, coming at the start, they do nothing that the text itself will not confirm or deny. Thus epigraphs become a kind of preparation for failure.

Or is the function of epigraphs to release metaphors and ideas from the bounds of a single time, place, and mind? Can quotation marks hold back a thought from seeking a larger identity in Thought? And of what are the walls within Language made?

These are questions that the im-mediate mind sometimes asks.

II. THE CONVERGENCE OF CONSCIOUSNESS

The theme of this

          paracritical essay

                    is   the growing
                    insistence of Mind

to apprehend reality im-mediately;

to gather more and more mind

                in itself:
                thus to become
                its own
                reality.

Consciousness becomes all.
And as in a gnostic
      dream,
            matter dissolves
                  before the
   Light.

Certainly, Consciousness has become one of our key terms, re-placing Honor, Faith, Reason, or Sensibility as the token of intellectual passion, the instrument of our cultural will. Cold-eyed behaviorists may eschew the term; yet its nimbus still hangs over our rhetoric as we discourse on politics and pornography, language and literature, morality and metaphysics. Thus we "raise," "expland," "alter," "criti-cize," and "bracket" consciousness, among so many other things we do to it nowadays.

This cultural chatter may not be wholly idle. A certain demate-rialization of our world is taking place, from the "etherealization" of culture (Arnold Toynbee) to the "ephemeralization" of substance (Buckminster Fuller) to the "de-definition" of art (Harold Rosenberg). The literary author "dies" (Roland Barthes), and the literary text van-ishes into a generic abstraction, *l'écriture*. How many forms, disci-plines, institutions, have we seen dissolve, in the last few decades, into amorphous new shapes? How many objects, solidly mattered, have we seen dissolve into a process, an image, a mental frame? "We are beyond space and time," John Brockman says in *Afterwords;* "we are beyond good and evil; there is only information; it is the control; the measure by which the operation of the brain changes. . . ." Dissolu-tion again?

The New York Times, *Oct. 22,*
1972:

The impact of the computer is felt in virtually every corner of Ameri-can life, from the ghetto to the moon. And data-processing is the world's fastest growing major busi-ness; sometime during the next

> *decace, it is expected to become*
> *the world's largest industry.*

From hardware to software, from software to pure mind?

Actually, the process may be one of convergence far more than of dissolution. The syntropic force of consciousness is remaking our world in every way. Thus Daniel Bell, like Buckminster Fuller, identifies the major source of transformation as "the exponential growth and branching of science, the rise of a new intellectual technology, the creation of systematic research . . . and, as the calyx of all this, the codification of theoretical knowledge" (*The Coming of the Post-Industrial Society*). The codification of theoretical knowledge unifies consciousness even as it enlarges it. Curiously, we are not far from Teilhard de Chardin, who said: "Everything that rises must converge." That is a hypothesis that we need, at least, to entertain.

Teilhard's famous phrase, however, provides Flannery O'Connor with an ironic title to a collection of stories. Why ironic? Because the stories reveal isolation, terror, and waste, reveal life without Grace. Here is another hypothesis of the human condition that we can not entirely repudiate. The radical insufficiency of that condition—I do not wish to say: of man—still offers intractable resistance to the old gnostic dream. Whether we call it evil, Ananke, or (mawkishly) The System, this resistance must be acknowledged. *Without assent.*

III. BEYOND ARCADIANS AND TECHNOPHILES

The New Gnosticism is the result of various synergies. Myth and Technology, for instance, now easily blend in the mind. A great part of our culture, however, still abets opposition, division. Consider, for instance, the current distinction between Arcadians and Technophiles:

The Arcadians look for the unspoiled life in nature. They tend to be mythically minded and edenic. Hostile to technology, they like communes, ecology, health foods, folk music, occult and visionary literature. They are children of the Earth, mother-oriented, ruled by the great archetypes. See Charles

The Technophiles favor the active life of cities. They tend to be technically minded and utopian. They like gadgets, science fiction, electronic music, space programs, futuristic designs of their environment. They are children of the Sky, father-oriented, struggling to create neo-types. See Zbigniew Brze-

Reich's *The Greening of America*, Theodore Roszak's *Where the Wasteland Ends*, or George B. Leonard's *The Transformation*.

zinsky's *Between Two Ages: America's Role in the Technetronic Era*, F. M. Esfandiary's *Optimism One: The Emerging Radicalism*, or Victor Ferkiss' *Technological Man*.

These, to be sure, are stereotypes. Yet their historic tensions inform such serious works as Leo Marx's *The Machine in the Garden*, Arthur Koestler's *The Ghost in the Machine*, and Lewis Mumford's *The Myth of the Machine*—note the titles—works that prefigure some of our postmodern perplexities.

Though the antipathy between Arcadians and Technophiles may derive from an ancient wound in the human psyche, there is nothing ineluctable about it. Earth and Sky, Myth and Technology have joined before and their gap is narrowing. Eden and Utopia, the first and last perfection, are homologous, imaginative constructs, mirror images of the same primal desire. Furthermore, the laws of myth and of science have this in common: both are partial codifications of reality, ways in which the mind imitates itself. Their structures, their functions, their predictive logic may not be identical; yet both are part of the human creative process. This assumption has led an eminent savant, Karl Friedrich von Weizsäcker, to explore the relation of yoga to physics at his institute near Munich. Again, neither myth nor science escapes the influence of the imagination. Einstein notes in *Ideas and Opinions*: "The axiomatic basis of theoretical physics cannot be extracted from experience, but must be freely invented." And J. Bronowski: "The step by which a new axiom is added cannot itself be mechanized. It is a free play of the mind, an invention outside the logical processes. This is the central act of imagination in science and it is in all respects like any similar act in literature" [*The American Scholar* (Spring, 1966)]. Why, then, should we wonder that Issac Newton labored secretly in alchemical pursuits, seeking the universal signature of life in all matter? And who knows what hieratic converse Newton carried on with Paracelsus across the centuries? And Kepler? The origins of mechanization are indeed more mystical than we suppose.*

That is a crucial intuition Arcadians tend to ignore—enough of dialectics; multilectics abound—even as they belabor Technophiles for

---

* Arthur Koestler's *The Roots of Coincidence* (1972) amplifies this point in interesting ways; regrettably, I read it after the completion of this essay.

their "single vision and Newton's sleep." Roszak's *Where the Waste-land Ends,* for instance, a work that engages some of my deepest sympathies, resolutely denies the potential of spiritual transformation contained in modern science. In so doing, it banishes imagination from a large area of consciousness, and evades the metaphysical meaning of change, innovation, and human evolution. I think it more likely that "mystics" and "mechanists," as William Irwin Thompson calls them, will move toward a new issue:

> Western civilization is drawing to a close in an age of apocalyptic turmoil in which the old species, collectivizing mankind with ma-chines, and the new species, unifying it in consciousness, are in collusion with one an-other to end what we know as human nature.
> (*At the Edge of History*)

But the convergence of which I speak manifests itself not only in broad cultural contexts; it finds a voice in private lives when least we expect it. Here is the late Jimi Hendrix:

> It's music. . . . It's electric-icity . . . that will take us all to that spiritual high I call the electric church. . . .
> Mind expansion . . . I expanded mine the first time I turned on and plugged into an electric amplifier . . . someday it's going to carry me all the way there, too: pure mind.
> (bibliographic reference lost)

The mythological bard becomes a technological mystic. Consider now a high-flier of a different kind, not a freaked-out black musician but a shy exemplar of WASP rectitude. Here is Charles Lindbergh:

> Gradually, I diverted hours from aviation into biological research. How mechanical, how mystical was man? Could longevity be extended? . . .
> Decades spent in contact with science and its vehicles have directed my mind and senses to areas beyond their reach. I now see scientific accomplishment as a path, not an end; a path leading to and disappearing in mystery.
> (*Life,* July 4, 1969)

Lindbergh, the romantic adventurer, evolves into a technocrat, and the technocrat soon becomes a nature mystic. Does his vision blend into that of Jimi Hendrix? And those astronauts who have returned from space to explore occult sciences, the inner matrix?

Admittedly, a few instances do not prove a trend. Yet the instances are scattered throughout our lives, as if each of us were compelled to discover his own Beulah, his own "place where Contrarieties are equally True." We have seen computer art aspire to Pythagorean mysteries. And even the dark avatars have disengaged themselves from our dreams to become, as in "2001: A Space Odyssey," technological prophecies.

The New Gnosticism eludes distinctions of the old mind, seeking yet unknown synergies.

Entropies:

Does the mind also create unknown entropies?
Ivan Karamazov: "It's not that I don't accept
God, you understand, it's the world created by
him that I don't accept."

        And still it seems the same:
        Death
           Dearth
               Deceit.

Everywhere the fullness of decay.

IV.   A DIGRESSION ON PROMETHEUS

Myth, Technology, and Literature meet in the various figures and fables of Prometheus.

As a Titan, Prometheus reverts to the chthonic forces of the Earth, of nature and instinct. Yet this Titan is clever; he allies himself with the new Parnassian order of Zeus. He reaches for the sky, and his name means foresight.

This Titan may be too clever. A natural trickster, he represents the creative principle of intelligence, creative yet essentially flawed because it is ignorant of its limit, its purpose. Prometheus begins lacking in wisdom.

Gaston Bachelard, The Psychoanalysis of Fire:
*This, then, is the true basis for the
respect shown to flame: if the child
brings his hand close to the fire his*

father raps him over the knuckles with a ruler. Fire, then, can strike without having to burn. Whether this fire be flame or heat, lamp or stove, the parents' vigilance is the same. Thus fire is initially the object of a general prohibition; *hence this conclusion: the social interdiction is our first* general knowledge of fire. . . . *Consequently, since the prohibitions are primarily social interdictions, the problem of obtaining a personal knowledge of fire is the problem of* clever disobedience. *The child wishes to do what his father does, but far away from his father's presence, and so like a little Prometheus he steals some matches.*

At Mecone, where gods and men come to settle their dispute, Prometheus tricks the gods of their share of the feast's meat. Henceforth, gods and men will stand apart. Prometheus defies Zeus again by bestowing fire on man, and bestowing mind (alphabet, number, all the practical and occult arts).

Prometheus: Titan of nature, creative Trickster, master of Technics. His sufferings begin. Perhaps he acquires dignity only on the terrible rock, spiked, chained, liver torn. Some say his torment is redemptive (Aeschylus), some say it proves only the absurdity of gods (Goethe). It is certain only that Prometheus suffers on Tartarus, and of his suffering creates an ambiguous prophecy. Or is it simply another trick? Probably not: this creature haruspicates with his own organs.

The prohecy promises—if you can penetrate it—deliverance:
Deliverance of Prometheus,
deliverance really of man.

Does it also promise the abolition
of the gods?
The matter is not yet clear.

Consider the Promethean fable in these texts:
A.   Hesiod's *Theogony, Works and Days*
B.   Aeschylus' *Prometheus Bound*

C. Goethe's *Prometheus: A Dramatic Fragment*
D. Percy Bysshe Shelley's *Prometheus Unbound*
E. Mary Shelley's *Frankenstein: or, The Modern Prometheus*
F. Gerald Feinberg's *The Prometheus Project*

At the origin there is an action: trickery, defiance, creation, hope, an alliance with man that defines the human condition in terms of limits and transgressions, lapses and transcendences. Fire is stolen, yes, and with it consciousness is wrested from its divine place. But like fire, consciousness is perverse; it seeks its solid opposite; and it devours its own pain. Released in the world, consciousness questions all, questions matter and every matter, vexing itself to the last. What, then, is the Promethean answer?

A. Hesiod largely reports the myth. Here and there he speaks with some didactic relish; but the redemption of Prometheus scarcely troubles his mind.

B. Aeschylus adheres to prophecy and patience. Let us wait for the advent of heroes (Herakles) who can mediate between men and gods, between death and eternity. But who are "heroes"? For us they are past; for Prometheus they are future. Or does Prometheus know some other secret about the end of Zeus?

C. Goethe thinks revolt. As C. K. Kerényi puts it: "Goethe's Prometheus is no God, no Titan, no man, but the immortal prototype of man as the original rebel and affirmer of his fate: the original inhabitant of the earth, seen as an antigod, as Lord of the Earth. In this connection he seems more Gnostic than Greek . . ." (*Prometheus: Archetypal Image of Human Existence*). Above all, he seems romantic and therefore nearly modern.

D. Percy Bysshe Shelley will not fully explain his Prometheus, a creature both of will and vision. Shelley sees him as kin to Milton's Satan, yet exempt from the "pernicious casuistry" of the rebel archangel. Bound by his own hate, by his own divided faculties, Prometheus strives to liberate himself from himself. To become whole again, he must find renewal in the Imagination. This Imagination is also teleological. At the end, Demogorgon assures Prometheus: ". . . to hope till Hope creates/From its own wreck the thing it contemplates / . . . This is alone Life, Joy, Empire, and Victory."

E.   Mary Shelley divines the point at which scientism and idealism, reason and revelation, meet. It is a point shrouded in terror. Frankenstein, the modern Prometheus, surrenders to Albertus Magnus and Paracelsus before he masters the exact sciences. "I was required," he says, "to exchange chimeras of boundless grandeur for realities of little worth." But his great error lies elsewhere. Self-absorbed and self-obsessed, he blights the powers of sympathy in himself. His solitary "fiend" returns to haunt him and haunt us, a ghastly embodiment of Prometheanism without responsibility or love. "Hateful day when I received life!" the fiend cries. Is that the curse of life born of pure mind? Frankenstein and his fiend are neither twain nor really one; but in this they are compact: both together adumbrate the perils of consciousness in its (heroic-demonic) labors of self-creation. This Promethean adventure ends in a world not of fire but of ice.

F.   Feinberg has fewer qualms about Prometheanism, about the increase of self-consciousness without bound. That increase is his project, and his Prometheus is ourselves. His premise is this: "My own feeling is that the despair of the conscious mind at the recognition of its own finitude is such that man cannot achieve an abiding contentment in his present form or anything like it. Therefore, I believe that a transformation of man into something very different from what he is now is called for." Calmly, lucidly, simplistically, Feinberg argues that mankind needs to set long-range ends for itself, and to devise corresponding means. The goal he proposes as the most likely human destiny is Promethean indeed: man will become a total consciousness. "Because of the inner logic of the conflict between the unity of one consciousness and the diversity of phenomena in the external world, there is probably no level of consciousness in which the conscious being will rest content until the sway of consciousness is extended indefinitely." We do not require the theology of Teilhard de Chardin to achieve this extension nor the science fiction of Olaf Stapledon. "I firmly believe," Feinberg notes, "that in trying to predict the future of technology, reality is likely to outstrip one's most extreme vision." The postmodern Prometheus reaches for the fire in distant stars.

The Promethean archetype (and I have left out many versions, including Gide's) is a focus of convergences that reappear in our midst. The archetype contains a gnostic dream or project:

the creation and continual re-creation

of human consciousness

until consciousness redeems itself in complete knowledge.

The Project implies will: Prometheus wills, and even wills to be wrong.

It implies also prophecy: Prometheus, that far-seer, falls forward into the fullness of time.

Above all,
it implies imagination :   Prometheus attempts a radical reconstitution of the given world, the fixed order of things.

Hence Prometheanism remains the arch human endeavor for that "visionary company" of poets about whom Harold Bloom has written vividly. Yes, there are acute dangers: solipsism, willfulness, self-corruption. Yet only in a spirit of extreme piety can we conclude, as William F. Lynch does in *Christ and Prometheus*, that "Prometheanism is the project of a will separated from the imagination and from reality, separated, therefore, from most of the human." Prometheanism, I think, veers toward the demonic when it denies the female principle of creation. Therefore, Aeschylus includes in his fable both Themis and Io, and Percy Shelley includes Asia. (Significantly, Mary Shelley's Frankenstein never consummates his relation to Elizabeth, nor is his relation to any man or woman but perfunctory.) There is a dark, moon-like side to Promethean nature, Kerényi insists, a side shaped by maternal forces. That side Prometheus can never afford to ignore.

No more than the Sky can ignore the Earth, or Technology, Mythology.

V. MYTH

I do not for a moment suggest that the New Gnosticism reverts directly to those ancient or medieval cults expounded, say, in Hans Jonas' excellent work, *The Gnostic Religion*. Still, new and old forms of gnosis may find a common source in certain myths, in certain persistencies of human dreams.

As in the beginning, so in the end; as above, so below. Such are the principles of mythical thought. Yet myth appears mainly retrograde, its focus on some event in the immemorial past, *in illo tempore.* Into that far, dim, and sacred time, a privileged state of existence is usually projected. Is that state one of universal consciousness?

We know the story of the Garden of Eden. There is also that other strange story in the Book of Genesis:

> And the whole earth was of one language and
> of one speech. . . .
> And they said, Go to, let us build us a city
> and a tower whose top may reach unto
> heaven. . . .
> And the Lord said, Behold, *the people is one,*
> *and they have all one language;* and this
> they begin to do: and now nothing will
> be restrained from them, which they
> have *imagined* to do.
> Go to, let us go down, and there confound
> their language, that they may not under-
> stand one another's speech (italics mine).

Just what was that unitary language of mankind before a jealous God struck it into a babel of tongues? Music? Mathematics? Telepathy? *Finnegans Wake?* Chomsky's deep structures of the mind or linquistic universals ringing each to each? Vico's primal language by mute religious acts?

Or was it the same language Orpheus spoke in distant Thrace, singing Orpheus, he who became himself bird and tree and rock and wolf and cloud? A poetry of silence? The silence of mind and nature when they perfectly meet? The silence that Norman O. Brown calls "the mother tongue?"

According to Erich Neumann, the ancient pleromatic or uroboric condition of existence is less conscious than unconscious, a state ruled by the Great Mother, a state, therefore, of *participation mystique.* Gnosticism, however, insists on spiritualizing this condition. "Consequently, in Gnosticism," Neumann says, "the way of salvation lies in heightening consciousness and returning to the transcendent spirit, with loss of the unconscious side; whereas uroboric salvation through the Great Mother demands the abandonment of the conscious principle and a homecoming to the unconscious" (*The Origins and History of Consciousness*).

The shift, then, seems to be from unconsciousness to consciousness. Teilhard agrees: "Mythology and folklore . . . are, in fact, filled with symbols and fables expressing the deeply rooted resolve of Earth to find its way to Heaven" (*The Future of Man*).

> *Joseph Campbell*, Psychology Today, *July, 1971, on the moon-walks:*
> *Now the earth has been elevated symbolically into the heavens, matter has been spiritualized . . . NASA has given us empirical proof that the only world we can experience is conditioned by the mathematics of space. So the old dichotomy between spirit and matter, God and man, is finished.*

Yet if Beginnings and Ends are cognate, they must express, on some concealed level at least, a point of contact, perhaps even of identity. In the Jewish *Midrash*, for instance, the unborn babe in its womb carries a prophetic light around its head in which it sees the end of the world. (Recall, again, the eschatological image of the luminous intergalactic foetus at the end of "2001.") Furthermore, the mystic trance and shamanistic journey are both ways of recovering the First and Last moment into the present.

Can it be, then, that the shift from unconsciousness to consciousness is true only in a partial perspective of reality? Can it be that conscious and unconscious are both implicit in the larger state of mind that myth projects far back into the sacred past and far forward into the sacred future? The state of mind that dream, vision, and trance recover in the im-mediate present?

> *Mircea Eliade*, Myths, Dreams, and Mysteries:
> *In India a whole literature has been devoted to explanations of this paradoxical relationship between what is pre-eminently unconscious—Matter—and pure "consciousness," the Spirit, which by its own mode of being is atemporal, free, uninvolved in the becoming. And one of the most unexpected results of this philosophic labor has been its conclu-*

> *sion that the Unconscious (i.e.*
> pakriti), *moving by a kind of*
> *"teleological instinct," imitates the*
> *behaviour of the Spirit; that the*
> *Unconscious behaves in such a way*
> *that its activity seems to* prefigure
> *the mode of being of the Spirit.*

I doubt that such questions can be answered at this time in any terms that would satisfy those who insist on an answer; yet they are the very questions that myth raises repeatedly before the skeptical mind. Behind these questions lurks a desire, an intuition, perhaps even a gnosis, of a universal consciousness that transcends time, and transcends the organization of our most complex language.

VI. TECHNOLOGY

We all acknowledge that science and its extension in technology are the major agents of transformation in our world. Sometimes we acknowledge it fearfully, and like Jacques Ellul in *The Technological Society,* we see only dark portents of our future. "Enclosed within his artificial creation," Ellul writes, "man finds that there is 'no exit'; that he cannot pierce the shell of technology to find again the ancient milieu to which he was adapted for hundreds of thousands of years." Certainly, anyone over thirty will remember that the earth was a cleaner place in the past, more surprising, and more sensuously various. Science and technology, however, also operate in other dimensions, silently, invisibly, making always a little more life available to us. Even a pessimist such as Ellul predicts: "There will be no need of attention or effort. What is needed will pass directly from the machine to the brain without going through consciousness."

Consider that familiar rubric, "the communication explosion." Quite precisely, a layer of sentience or awareness now envelops the earth, much like Teilhard's "noösphere," moving ever

Query

> The communication explosion is a product not only of technology but also of the population explosion. There are, literally, more brains on earth, working all at the same time. How does this fact affect the degree of sentience on earth?

End of Query

outwards. Furthermore, communication itself is becoming increasingly immediate, requiring less and less mediation. It is a far cry from a stone hieroglyph weighing fifty tons to a wireless set weighing less than a pound. Even now we casually use "slow-motion telepathy," as Barry Schwartz puts it, devices that require only microseconds to elapse between coded communication, decoded message, and feedback [*Arts in Society* (Summer-Fall, 1972)]. The process can be extended by radio or laser far into the universe. There are also other means.

> The New York Times, *Feb. 27, 1972:*
>
> *Tonight, if all goes well, the United States will launch the longest space mission in history. . . . It is the first official effort of mankind to draw attention to itself. As the vehicle, Pioneer 10, passes Jupiter, the gravity of that planet will seize it and hurl it out of the solar system. It will sail indefinitely through the vast reaches of the Milky Way Galaxy, carrying a message. . . .*
>
> The message is not composed of quotations from Shakespeare. It includes visual representations of the male and female figures, and mathematical symbols referring to the structure of the hydrogen molecule and the frequency of pulsars. Can the basic rhythms of the universe provide a Pythagorean alphabet of universal intelligence?

Matter is giving way. As Buckminster Fuller puts it in *Intuiton:*

> In short, physics has discovered
> That there are no solids,
> No continuous surfaces,
> No straight lines;
> Only waves,
> No things,
> Only energy *event* complexes,
> Only behaviors,
> Only verbs,
> Only relationships. . . .

This discovery bolsters the process of "ephemeralization": doing constantly more with constantly less. As a result, matter intervenes less and less in the transactions of mankind. And mind is free to pursue its destiny: to become the antientropic, or syntropic, force in the universe, gathering knowledge, expanding consciousness, regenerating *metaphysically* a *physically* decaying universe. In this ambience of sentience, telepathy becomes a new possibility. Thus Fuller again: "I think that possibly within ten years we'll discover scientifically that what has been telepathy and has been thought of as very mysterious is, in fact, ultra, ultra, high frequency electromagnetic wave propagation" (*House and Garden,* May, 1972).

Telepathy, the gnostic language, in technology?

A. In 1954, Norbert Wiener, father of cybernetics, said in his book, *The Human Use of Human Beings:*

> Let us admit that the idea that one might
> conceivably travel by telegraph, in addition
> to traveling by train or airplane, is not intrin-
> sically absurd, far as it may be from realiza-
> tion.

Within two decades, we hear that Japanese researchers are trying to develop "Intersex" or "Cybersex": long-distance sex between consenting partners. The idea is to record as fully as possible—oh, much more than Masters and Johnson ever dreamed—all sexual stimuli, visual, tactile, auditory, olfactory, and even kinetic, and to transmit these stimuli, through electronic devices and computers, to sexual partners. Furthermore: "By the end of the century, Hikari expects to see commercial Cybersex tapes, recorded by prominent male and female celebrities, generally available, much as one buys a phonograph recording today" (*Architectural Design,* September, 1969).

B. In 1964, Marshall McLuhan stated in his book *Understanding Media:*

> Electric technology does not need words any
> more than the digital computer needs num-
> bers. Electricity points the way to an exten-
> sion of the process of consciousness itself, on
> a world scale, and without any verbalization
> whatever.

Within less than a decade, we hear that Dr. José Delgado at Yale has implanted electrodes in special brain areas of a fighting bull. By pushing a button, he was able to stop the bull in the middle of the fiercest charge. There is nothing to prevent Dr. Delgado from "wiring" his bull to a computer, and programming its existence. There is no theoretical difficulty to prevent us from doing the same thing with human beings, as the television program "Search" weekly suggests to oblivious audiences. "Soon," Dr. Delgado says, "with the aid of the computer, we may have direct contact between two different brains—without the participation of the senses" (*The New York Times Magazine*, November 15, 1970). Soon, too, with the aid of "Dream Machines" acting directly on the brain, we may simulate, we may *possess*, any sensuous experience while sitting at home: a three-star meal at Lasserre in Paris or free-fall from a plane over the Andes.

We can imagine the utopian and dystopian possibilities of these and other developments; indeed, many of them have been imagined already in science fiction. Yet a hysterical rejection of science and its applications will not do; for there is no way for us to repress what we already know, what we already are and can be, without grave consequences to our psychic health. We must find a way to restore the deep rhythms of life within us without forgoing the dream that may be leaving its imprint—a biological code?—on our evolution.

Already, our senses are becoming coextensive with the cosmos: we can "touch" things on the moon and "hear" quasars at the edge of the universe. Slowly, we are all entering a multi-dimensional, non-Euclidean, and still sensuous—for sense and mind are one—realm of existence. We can begin to "speak" to one another, and to the animals at hand, as well as to invite, as we have done, voices farther out in space to speak to us.

> *John C. Lilly*, Man and Dolphin:
> *Within the next decade or two the human species will establish communication with another species: nonhuman, alien, possibly extraterrestrial, more probably marine; but definitely highly intelligent, perhaps even intellectual. . . .*
> *Our own spot in the universe, our own view of ourselves, will be tremendously modified if such a communication is established. Any other species that could talk with us on our own level will give us a*

*perspective of which we can only
be dimly aware at the present
time. Our own communication
among ourselves will be enhanced
and improved by such contact.
Our own views of one another will
change radically under the influence of interspecies communication. The very fact that we try to
communicate with them is an important indication of our own stage
of evolutionary maturity.*

We can further insist that technology become not only pollution-free
but also invisible. There are those who believe that technology can
imitate the inherent order of things. Here, for instance, is John Cage:

> Just as Fuller domes (dome within dome,
> translucent, plants between) will give impres-
> sion of living in no home at all (outdoors), so
> all technology must move toward way things
> were before man began changing them: iden-
> tification with nature in her manner of opera-
> tion, complete mystery.
>
> (*A Year from Monday*)

In short, like Myth, Technology suggests that man is creating a
universal consciousness which renders mediated action and speech
gradually obsolete. A measure of radical American Innocence is required to hold this view. Cage has it. So has Charles Lindbergh, who
may be even a greater technological gnostic:

> Will we discover that only *without* spaceships
> can we reach the galaxies; that only *without*
> cyclotrons can we know the interior of atoms?
>
> (*Life*, July 4, 1969)

Jonathan Livingston Seagull speaking?

VII. LITERATURE

Men of letters tend to believe that the word gives the mind its
flesh; and critics are even more stringent than the authors they criti-
cize in defense of that view. Literature is the keystone of the humanities; it stands, like Man, between Earth and Sky, severed from neither.
We expect it, therefore, to show a certain recalcitrance toward the
im-mediate mind.

Yet there are signal exceptions. Giordano Bruno, for instance: "The actual and the possible are not different in eternity." Or William Blake: "Mental Things are alone Real; what is called Corporeal, Nobody knows of its Dwelling Place: it is in Fallacy, & its Existence an Imposture . . ." ("A Vision of the Last Judgment"). Curiously enough, Blake's contemporary, Donatien Alphonse François de Sade, would have agreed entirely, for reasons demoniac of his own. One is tempted to argue—as I have in *The Dismemberment of Orpheus*—that Blake and Sade stand at the threshold of the modern experience, exemplars of two kinds of gnosticism. But there are, of course, other kinds; the gnostic impulse, restricted as it may be in literature, touches visionary, antinomian, or romantic writers of every age.

The unmediated will, however, asserts itself as a cultural phenomenon in the late eighteenth century. The artist begins his journey to the interior, there to end by discovering the languages of silence. Hegel provides Romanticism with a point of philosophical reference, and also of reaction.

> *Erich Heller,* The Artist's Journey into the Interior:
>
> *In both the early Romantics and Hegel, the human mind puts forward a total claim for itself, a claim in which revolution and eschatology are uneasily mingled. The world must become imagination and poetry, say the Romantics; and Hegel says, the world must become rational consciousness. But the poetry meant by the Romantics, and the rational consciousness meant by Hegel, have much in common: above all the ambition of the human mind to dominate the real world to the point of usurping its place.*

The world becomes poetry even as the final unfolding of the World-Spirit makes all poetry redundant, all art obsolete. That is the paradoxical prophecy of the Romantic "soul."

The journey into the interior is a journey toward consciousness, toward mind claiming more and more for itself in terms less and less conditional. It is a gnostic journey only in the very broadest sense, and its shadowy paths may be discerned in various human endeavors. Philosophy, for instance, moving from Hegel to Heidegger, Husserl, Sartre, and Wittgenstein, finds itself in an immense new field of subjectivity which it hopelessly sets out to survey. Literary criticism follows a similar path in the different works of Poulet, Blanchot, Barthes, Foucault, Derrida, a path that leaves "texts" behind, wanders brilliantly through language, and vanishes finally into consciousness.

As for literature itself, we have heard its story told many times, going as far back as Erich Kahler does in *The Inward Turn of Narrative,* or as far forward as Sharon Spencer in *Space, Time and Structure in the Modern Novel.* From the great modernists—Valéry, Proust, Rilke, Kafka, Joyce, Yeats, Pound, Eliot, Stevens, etc.—to the enigmatic postmodernists—Beckett, Borges, Genet, Butor, Cortazar, Barth, etc.—the tendency of literature has been to escape itself, to subvert or transcend its forms, to re-imagine imagination; and, as it were, to create a state of unmediated literary awareness. Yet a generalization of this kind cries for qualifications that I can scarcely begin to make here. We need a narrower focus: not gnostic tendencies in their shadowy outlines but the New Gnosticism in American literature particularly. This will bring us eventually to science fiction.

An Aside: Burroughs and Others

Ever since *Naked Lunch,* William Burroughs has declared himself, in words certainly, the enemy of language: "To speak is to lie"; "Rub out the Word Forever." Or in *The Ticket That Exploded:* "The word is now a virus. . . . The word may once have been a healthy neural cell. It is now a parasitic organism that invades and damages the central nervous system. Modern man has lost the option of silence."

Burroughs' icy rage against language is partly self-parodic. But it is also directed against the Old Consciousness, all its deceptions, inhibitions, and controls, which he identifies with the Word. Above all, his aversion sustains a failed dream of pure consciousness. "Words —at least the way we use them—can stand in the way of what I call non-body experience," he says. "It's time we thought about leaving the body behind" (*Writers at Work: The Paris Review Interviews, Third Series*). And leaving also the earth behind, Burroughs insists; for in doing so, we gain a new perspective on our conditioned existence, on the meaning of gravity. Burroughs, then, is a technological gnostic; quite explicitly, he hopes that science will help to remake man. Autonomic processes, hallucinogenic drugs, electric stimulation of the brain, telepathy and telekinesis—all these interest him because they exercise the powers of the mind to transform itself, to act directly upon itself without tiresome interventions of body or matter ("Interview," *Penthouse*, March, 1972).

But is the case of Burroughs relevant to our general cultural condition, or is it simply a terminal case of literature? The answer, I suspect, depends on how we value other writers, mentalists all of different kinds. In the background stands Wallace Stevens: "Modern reality is a reality of decreation, in which our revelations are not the revelations of belief, but the precious portents of our own powers. The greatest truth we could hope to discover . . . is that man's truth is the final resolution of everything." Closer to us stand Nabokov, Beckett, Borges. And closer still, consider the playful "ultimacy" of John Barth's *Chimera;* the entropic indeterminacy of Thomas Pynchon's *The Crying of Lot 49;* the pop or "dreck" surrealism of Donald Barthelme's *City Life;* the oneiric death-denying abandon of Robert Coover's *The Universal Baseball Association;* the epistemological introversion of Rudolph Wurlitzer's *Flats;* the self-reflexive exuberance of Raymond Federman's *Double or Nothing* and its typographic laughter; and the regenerative narrative blanks of Ronald Sukenick's *Out.* Admittedly these fictions are distinct, and their postmodern authors even more so. But do not these authors share with Burroughs a complex desire to dissolve the world—or at least to recognize its dissolution—and to remake it as an absurd or decaying or parodic or private—*and still imaginative*—construct? Geomancers more than mystics, they still abolish the terror, dreariness, and hazards of given things by FANTASY. Is this FANTASY, then, a novel type of secular gnosis? Perhaps like that "obscure man" in Borges' "The Circular Ruins," we all dream our successor into being. Perhaps we need a still narrower focus.

> *Ronald Sukenick*, The Death of the Novel and Other Stories:
> *The contemporary writer—the writer who is acutely in touch with the life of which he is part—is forced to start from scratch: Reality doesn't exist, time doesn't exist, personality doesn't exist. God was the omniscient author, but he died; now no one knows the plot,*

and since our reality lacks the
sanction of a creator, there's no
guarantee as to the authenticity of
the received version.
Also quoted in Jerome Klinkowitz
& John Somer, eds., Innovative
Fiction: Stories for the Seventies.

XIII. SCIENCE FICTION

A sharper view of the New Gnosticism in American literature
would focus on science fiction. This may appear the easy way out of
certain cultural and aesthetic complexities. Yet it is right for us to be
curious about science fiction at this time. It is the imaginative form
that creates new myths of our machines, new models of our social
existence, new images of our destiny in the universe. As fable, as
satire, as prophecy, then, the best science fiction deserves a quality of
critical attention that we have tended to deny it. This attention may
be forthcoming, particularly since so many "serious" novelists—as
different from one another as Burgess, Burroughs, and Vonnegut—are
finding the genre congenial.

And here is the point: some of the finest science fiction concerns
itself, like its two parents, Myth and Technology, with the question
of a universal consciousness. Sometimes the assumption appears to be
that wherever life obtains in heightened forms, intelligence also functions in im-mediate ways. At other times, the assumption is simply
that human minds are good enough to imagine better minds with,
but good for little more.

European science fiction has richly rendered its own versions of
this theme (see Fred Hoyle's *The Black Cloud,* Olaf Stapledon's *Last
and First Men,* and Stanislaw Lem's *Solaris*). My examples, however,
will refer to four works that are part of the American scene.

A. Robert Heinlein's *Stranger in a Strange Land*
B. Alfred Bester's *The Demolished Man*
C. Theodore Sturgeon's *More Than Human*
D. Ursula LeGuin's *The Lathe of Heaven*

A. There are rumors that Heinlein's famous work, full of dull
and jolly claptrap, has influenced the commune of Charles Manson.
But the erotic and religious cults that fill the novel are less crucial

than the "grokking" powers of its presumably Martian hero. These cults reveal that Earthlings are still corporeal, that their imperfect grokking faculties must be mediated mystically through the flesh. Grokking itself means complete identification, total understanding, a momentary fusion of two beings into a larger awareness. The concept carries the mythic feeling of *participation mystique* and the technological idea of telepathy to their point of contact.

B.   Bester's novel shows that in some distant future the fate of the human race depends on a nearly incorruptible society of mind readers, called "Espers" or, colloquially, "peepers." Third-class peepers can penetrate the conscious mind of "normals"; second-class, the preconscious mind; and first-class, the deep subconscious. But the whole society of mind readers constitutes a link with the future development of man, his evolution toward a larger consciousness. When a powerful, egotistic, and homicidal tycoon threatens this evolution, his "normal" brain is flooded with the collective psychic energy of all the peepers. Thus he receives illumination, perceives the mystery of his own identity and of cosmic love. He is "demolished" only as a willful and isolate self, caged in its obsolete needs.

C.   But the most subtle of these science fictions may be Sturgeon's. The time is the present; somewhere in the woods of America a community accidentally takes shape. This community is composed of a grown telepathic idiot; twin little black girls who are teleports; a slightly older white telekineticist; and her charge, a mongoloid infant with the mind of a computer and extraterrestrial connections. Solitary and freakish apart, together they form a preternatural organism, a new kind of intelligent life, called *homo gestalt,* that also possesses the means to conquer gravity. "Gravitics," it seems, would add Psyche to the Unified Field that already includes Matter, Energy, Space, and Time. But as it turns out, *homo gestalt* must learn from *homo sapiens* something about a moral ethos before making its quantum spiritual jump.

D.   Dreams create and literally re-create reality, which may itself be the final version of dream, in *The Lathe of Heaven.* The year is around 2002. Under the hypnotic influence of Dr. Haber and his electric Augmentor, Orr is made to dream utopia. Orr's dreams "solve" the problems of population, pollution, war, and race; these dreams expunge six billion people and convert an alien race of galactic invaders into wise allies. Yet somehow things always get a little worse after each of these effective and retroactive dreams. For the central argument of the book is between Being and Becoming, Change and Still-ness. Orr's dreams, as the aliens teach him, are part of a cosmic, will-less, incommunicable force: "Everything dreams. The play of form, of being, is the dreaming of substance. . . . But when the mind be-comes conscious, when the rate of evolution speeds up, then you have to be careful." The cautionary note is struck by Chuang Tse in an epigraph: "To let understanding stop at what cannot be understood is a high attainment. Those who cannot do it will be destroyed on the lathe of heaven." So much for the omnipotence of mind.

These four science fictions are by no means unique in presaging —and warning against!—the transformation of man into a vast noetic reality, a universal consciousness capable of im-mediate exchanges of knowledge. Can such anticipatory myths become slow, self-fulfilling prophecies? Or is the future simply our most widely shared, treasured, and revised fantasy?

IX.   CODA

Once again, I should stress that I am not concerned here with the old Gnostic religions, their theories of creation and apocalypse, their dualisms and demiurges, their Elohims, Sophias, Abraxas, and Helens. I am concerned, however, with a new sense of the im-mediacy of Mind, of complete gnosis or knowledge. This sense implies a vast, new role of Consciousness in the universe. The role was vaguely pre-figured by the ancient Gnostics, authors of a passionate subjectivity.

But the New Gnosticism does not rest only on mystical experi-ences or mythical archetypes; it insinuates itself into postmodern literature; and it appears as a condition of our science, of our tech-nology. The New Gnosticism, in fact, presupposes convergences that are silently altering the definitions of culture.

> (Brown's mythical vision of poly-morphous perversity and Mc-Luhan's technological idea of elec-tricity as a human nervous system both decenter the ego and diffuse the brain; and Marcuse's new Reality Principle assumes an order "under which a new sensibility and

a desublimated scientific intelligence would combine in the creation of an *aesthetic ethos*.")

Will such convergences end by changing the definitions of man?

I have spoken in a speculative voice. I have assumed, as some others have, that we are witnessing a radical transformation of man. But there are alternatives to this assumption. We may, for instance, obliterate ourselves as a race. Or we may develop apace, doing more or less what we do now, without any radical change in our destiny. Or again, we may indeed change radically in a way that entails no universal consciousness. Everything that rises must converge? Perhaps it is also everything that falls.

I have spoken in a speculative voice to raise questions, not to foreclose them; but speculations may also clear the way for theory, judgment, or belief. No doubt every reader will have his responses. The questions that remain concern us, more specifically, as readers and writers of literature. How shall we respond to these new realities? Should we sever ourselves from the sources of imagination and change in our time? Can we enter the gnostic dream to give it a larger and richer shape? Or will we continue to sustain ourselves on our own traditions, with piety, skepticism, and complex hope?

An Exemplum: Norman Mailer

He has always strained to become exemplary in America. His home, we know, is the domain of the Self: power, instinct, vision. Closer to the old magic than to the new, he has been a deep and ambiguous critic of technology. Yet here, perhaps, is a failure: he conceals from himself what I think he senses, that magic and technology meet at a vital point in human evolution. Mailer, at any rate, sees that shamans and computers enjoy their intercourse in the surreal world of today and tomorrow:

> Yet even this model of the future was too simple. For the society of the rational and the world of the irrational would be without boundaries. Computersville had no cure for skin disease but filth in the wound, and the guru had no remedy for insomnia but a trip to the moon, so people would be forever migrating between the societies. Sex would be a

new form of currency in both worlds—on that
you could count.

(*Of a Fire on the Moon*)

Sex—and also its primordial equivalents, Gravity and Light? Who
knows what the sexual consciousness—body seeking body, energy
freed from itself—might become?

The example Mailer sets before the community of letters is that
of its own endeavor, that of the literary act itself, in our time. His
vaulting ambition, imagination, irony attempt to comprehend some
final facts and fancies of the age. But the recalcitrance of our palpable life, the persistence of our prejudice and pain, contrast so sharply
with the invisible possibilities of the human race that even the most
extreme vision must hedge itself. In our quotidian existence, hunger
and anger still rule the day far more than imagination prevails.

End of Exemplum

The New Gnosticism assumes that the more consciousness increases, the more Fact and Fancy will converge, the more Is and Can,
Sensation and Thought, become one. The Literary Imagination can
only hold the New Gnosticism in suspicion; the latter doubts that
Imagination will still find its primary fulfillment in Literature.

Quite probably the great chain of being, extending from hell to
heaven, running through all the intermediate forms of creation, is
broken. Or more precisely: the great chain of being is reconstituting
itself in one great link or loop of consciousness, not linear but multi-
form. Men and Women no longer stand between Earth and Sky; they
are becoming both and either.

Yet how many
     within or without
     academies of mind
          of every kind
can truly perceive
     where this metaphor
     of our friend   (Blake)
        ends?
         (Not I).

    . . . each grain of Sand,
  Every stone on the land,

Each rock & each hill,
Each fountain & rill,
Each herb & each tree,
Mountain, hill, earth, & sea,
Cloud, Meteor, & Star,
Are Men Seen Afar.

* Epigraph references: *The Tibetan Book of the Dead; The Gospel of Truth;* William Blake, *Jerusalem;* Ralph Waldo Emerson, *Nature;* Henri Bergson, *The Two Sources of Morality and Religion;* Sir James Jeans, *The Mysterious Universe;* Teilhard de Chardin, *Building the Earth;* Marshall McLuhan, *Understanding Media;* R. Buckminster Fuller, *Intuition;* Gerald Feinberg, *The Prometheus Project;* Norman O. Brown, *Love's Body;* Louis Kahn, *Time,* January 15, 1973.

MODELS OF TRANSFORMATION:
Ideology, Utopia, and Fantasy in America

I. SLEEP

Every age seems the best of times and the worst of times. Some ages engage in re-revolution; others re-cover rumors of some utopia or eden. But our intelligence remains rooted in the Human: brain soil, sun fire, old dark matter of the heart. Can anything really change? Myself, I believe in a transformation of man more radical than any Darwin, Marx, Freud, and even Einstein could foresee. This transformation appears both sudden and immeasurably slow. One or two or three million years ago, the human brain exploded into biological evolution. Awkwardly erect, a new creature began to roam the earth, of nature the latest born. *Homo sapiens, homo magus, homo faber, homo ludens, homo progressivus:* our prejudices have bestowed on him many names. Yet he emerges as the self-transforming animal, self-destructive but self-transcending too. This power of transformation may well have been rooted in his sleep. Prehistoric man slept and slept, Lewis Mumford speculates, and during long hours he dreamed. The dreaming animal, floating between his inner and outer worlds, began to weave the web of consciousness, of his language, culture, and technics. Creativity began in the deep. Thus, paradoxically, "it was the dream that opened man's eyes to new possibilities in his waking life," Mumford concludes. Yet dreams also open on the future. Does the transformation of man renew itself continually in this struggle between waking and dreaming?

> *Proposition I*
> *Ideology, Utopia, and Fantasy: agents of change, quests for new reality, memories of a Dream.*

151

II. FOR A THEORY OF CHANGE

We have no adequate, no truly contemporary, theory of change. Not since Marx, I think, and his no longer suffices. There have been attempts. Psychoanalysis sought new relations between wakefulness and dream, between man and child. Existentialism developed a metaphysics of self-creation. Science evoked paradigms of innovation. Still, no theory of change. Currently, the dominant influences of Structuralism, Phenomenology, the New Linguistics, favor not change but codes, patterns, deep forms through which the mind, as Lévi-Strauss put it, "imitates itself"; we move among crystals, mirrors and crystals.

> The question remains: is the Universe given or still in the making? Wherewhen Being and Becoming converge? And what do we mean by Change?
>
> A theory of deep forms may make the idea of change itself obsolete: Plato's dream.
>
> Or is there, instead, a point beyond all our structures, where matter, life, and consciousness do meet?
>
> A gamma or galaxy, breath or death, symbols dancing in the mind, may all possess some common ordinance.

Though I have no proposal for an adequate theory of change, I have some sense of its rudiments, its aspirations. Such a theory would:

a– acknowledge *the equivocal dynamism of the Western mind* since pre-Socratic philosophers: Heraclitus, who thought that reality, like an ever-living fire, dies and rekindles itself again; Pythagoras, who thought that spirit, though passing to ever-changing bodies, remains always the same;

b– recognize that *change has become intrinsic to the human condition.* Increasingly, the slogan "innovate or die" appears as the principle of our still-random evolution, full of errors, adaptations, and miraculous mutations;

c– understand that *true change is ultimately creation and surprise.* Daniel Bell does not go far enough: "The function of prediction is not, as often stated, to aid social control, but to widen the spheres of moral choice." Rather Dennis Gabor: "The future cannot be predicted, but futures can be invented";

d– yet still inquire into *all the means and aims of transformation available to human kind,* asking in particular: how are neotypes of archetypes made? how may we alter the old structure of mental and physical heredity and to what end? Here all disciplines, from ethics to futuristics, have their say;

e— and also wonder: *is there a special destiny for man?* a particular meaning to his evolution among species? a unique quality in the momentum he generates in the universe? Here dream, myth, and art join their gaity to science;

f— meantime, accept *the global frame of human endeavor,* the commitment to global problems and global solutions; no part of the earth can now escape the influence of another, and all minds begin to interplay (see Section III below);

g— admit, finally, that any powerful theory of change soon becomes a myth of change, a structure of beliefs, a dogma. Thus a truly adequate theory *must prove its own ability to change;* it must possess the potency to expire.

I am aware of the inner contradictions in some of these requirements, the tensions that a theory of change must perpetuate till it declares itself obsolete. They are the contradictions of our consciousness, and we escape them only at the point where consciousness either diminishes or increases toward a new consciousness.

> Theoreticians of change! let us ponder how we may assent to Nietzsche and still refute him when he cries: "Live so that thou mayest desire to live again,—that is thy duty,—for in any case thou wilt live again."

III. THE MACHINE FOR GODS

Henri Bergson concludes *The Two Sources of Morality and Religion* by appealing to the human race "to make just the extra effort required for fullfilling, even on their refractory planet, the essential function of the universe, which is a machine for the making of gods." Bergsonian optimism? Perhaps. Yet the appeal still sounds in a world that knows far more about error and menace than he could foresee in 1932. The appeal still sounds in American popular culture as well as in the high, intellectual tradition of Bergson's France:

Stewart Brand: "We are as gods and may as well get good at it."
Jean-Paul Sartre: "Man is the project of becoming god."

And with another emphasis:

> Pogo: "We have met the enemy and he is us."
>
> Claude Lévi-Strauss: "The words 'reactionary' and 'revolutionary' have meaning only in terms of conflicts which pit one group of men against another. Today, however, the great peril to mankind does not stem from the actions of one regime, party, group, or class. Rather, it is the family of man itself which poses that threat, exposed as its own worst enemy and at the same time, alas, as the worst enemy of the rest of creation."

George Kateb states the matter plainly: "To conceive of the revolution in human capacities as an acquisition of God-like powers is simply a clumsily unoriginal shorthand way of indicating the emergent redefinition of man." But our mutual friend, the Realist within, may put it even more plainly. "That's all very well," he growls, "but most of us have not felt very omnipotent lately. What's more, godlike powers create god-awful problems. Just take a look around you—or haven't you been out of the Ivory Tower in a while? And what makes you think, anyway, that god-like powers are needed to solve particular human problems?" This Realist can turn sour.

With some reason. The discrepancy between the potential and the reality of change in our time contributes greatly to our anger, alienation, anomie. We are assured that dearth has been conquered while men starve before our eyes, that war and terror have become obsolete while men kill and torture every day, that love, liberty, and the pursuit of happiness are within our grasp while divorce, addiction, suicide, and madness rule the statistics of every "advanced" society.

Yet the choice is no longer between rubrics: realist or idealist, activist or visionary. When change is so rapid and so crucial, all rubrics must inhabit the same flesh. Else the activist becomes a figure of spite, the visionary a creature of futility. Ontological divisions—do they always revert to Self and Other, Us and Them?—become epistemological lesions. The time of fragmentary beings may be near its end; for consciousness is becoming as wide as life.

Thus, about the "machine for gods," we may say:

> *Proposition II*
> *Mankind henceforth takes responsibility for*
> *its destiny as a single unit of Consciousness.*
> *When responsibility becomes total, so does*

power. Divine responsibility, demonic
power: both obsolete. Will they vanish into
a new concept of Love?

Meanwhile, we have the new new politics?

> Bobby Seale, mayoral candidate in Oakland, 1972:
> "The Black Panther Party is not a separatist party.
> We believe that it's a natural law of the universe
> that everything is interconnected and becoming
> more so because of the advancements of tech-
> nology. As victims of racism, we won't take up
> that banner."

IV. A DIGRESSION: ON LITERATURE, POLITICS, AND CHANGE

Ideology, Utopia, and Fantasy may be agents of change. They are also forms of Literature. But what of literature in its more classic sense, as "serious" fiction, poetry, drama? What pressures can that literature exert on change?

On this topic, literary men rarely agree. There have been ambitious moments. Shelley, for instance, claimed for poets the power of "unacknowledged legislators of the race." This has changed. Auden admitted that "in the case of any really serious social evil, it is conceit and absolute folly for poets to imagine that writing poems about it they are going to change things." And even Sartre, embattled *philosophe*, sadly concludes in his autobiography: "For a long time, I took my pen for a sword; I know now we're powerless."

And what of the politics of the great modernist authors: Yeats, Pound, Rilke, Eliot, Claudel, Lawrence, Proust, Faulkner, Wyndham Lewis? Reactionaries, pseudo-aristocrats, and some even crypto-fascists? This has led as cautious a critic as Frank Kermode to say, "There may even be a real relation between certain kinds of effectiveness in literature and totalitarianism in politics." Mann, Hemingway, or Gide may have been exceptions; but few others among the early modernists were actively libertarian. Admittedly, the second world war modified the relation between literature and politics; from Brecht and Camus to Grass and Mailer, two generations of writers learned to live closer to history. Still, considering the century as a whole, literary experimenters seldom seem revolutionary in politics, nor do engaged authors often submit to a party's discipline.

The relation of literature to progress, perhaps to everything public, whether ethical or politic, remains ambiguous. This ambiguity casts a long shadow on culture. Just how deeply does literature humanize, George Steiner asked, recollecting those camp commandants who, as everyone by now surely knows, loved Shakespeare, Goethe, and Rilke? The question returned to vex us at the center of another controversy, initiated by C. P. Snow and F. R. Leavis; and still it persists in new forms as technophiles and technophobes of our day debate the miseries of our environment. Indeed, the question penetrated our universities. Students challenged the relevance of literary studies in the classroom even as a president of the Modern Language Association threw his gauntlet before the assembled scholars.

> *Note:* In the wake of the Snow-Leavis controversy, G. S. Fraser suggested that the human world would not be saved by "teaching English at universities." Lionel Trilling rebuked Fraser: "No, the world will not be saved by teaching English at universities, nor, indeed, by any other literary activity," and went on to make another point about the reality of politics. Yet both Fraser and Trilling miss the fact that the explosion of knowledge in our century has compelled universities to become powerful instruments of cultural change. Natural scientists and most social scientists realize this fact; see, for instance, Daniel Bell, *The Coming of the Post-Industrial Society.* But few humanists concern themselves with the question. Oddly enough, a mythographer, Northrop Frye, seems to be among those few. In *The Modern Century,* he argues that the spheres of education, leisure, and cultural influence have become interlocked.

Everywhere, radical authors both white and black struggle to keep their art alive between the demands of hope and outrage. Some, like the French authors of *Tel Quel,* separate politics entirely from literature; while others, like the Afro-Americans of Spirit House, attempt to fuse both politics and literature. Yet neither the refusals of the ones nor the advocacies of the others can conceal the ambiguities of their role, the agonies of their art. It is almost too easy to conclude that literature must remain an eccentric force, a perverse element, in human evolution.

A Paragon of Perversity
Jean Genet, pariah, thief, artist. His biography re-

veals Nothing; like Sade, he invents his true biography within black prison walls. Gradually, the life emerges, a complete artifice, synthetic flower of evil, one more object to wither in the sun.

Politics and literature? Genet visits the Sorbonne in May, 1968. Students greet his oblique appearance with applause. He says: "I refuse all complicity in the establishment of a new order. Everything that I have seen here gets me worried. The whole thing stinks of glue. . . ." He disappears. But the same year, *Esquire* persuades him to cover the Democratic National Convention. Genet comments on the massive thighs of Chicago policemen.

Eroticism, politics, and literature? Black is Beautiful. Genet lectures in America to raise funds for Bobby Seale and Huey Newton and writes an introduction to George Jackson's *Soledad Brother*: "The extravagant adventure of white America . . . is doubtless exhausted, it will dissolve and fade, revealing at last what is cheerfully devouring it: the black nation which was caught within it, itself traversed by liberating currents . . . producing long screams of misery and joy." But this is also the author of *Funeral Rites,* heavy with the poetry of death and Nazism.

In the end, neither power nor politics, neither crime nor eroticism, can rival poetry which "contains both the possibility of a revolutionary morality and what appears to contradict it"—contains really the void. Genet follows the inhuman to the edge, hopes for an apocalypse of absence. Love, politics, and morality dissolve into poetry; poetry dissolves into Nothing.

The case of Genet may be dismissed as an extreme case of modern alienation in the West. This may well be so. More than in any other century, our arts claim the muse of a conscious Negativity. Yet in doing so, they imply Positivity as well: the silence of emptiness summons a silent fullness from afar. Even Jean Genet secretly, ever so secretly, hopes that Evil may usher a new order in. Other artists, contemporaries and precursors, have been less rigorous in their despair; and some have proclaimed their hopes for mankind loudly.

Note: We may read their story in Donald Drew Egbert's *Social Radicalism and the Arts,* a cultural history of Western Europe from the French Revolution to 1968; or review the problematics of the subject in "Literature and Revolution," *Tri-Quarterly* (Winter-Spring, 1972); "Ideology and Literature," *New Literary History* (Spring, 1973); and "The Humanist Alternative," *Arts in Society* (Spring-Summer, 1973).

Thus the ambiguity of literature continues, teasing our sense of the future, denying our presence and affirming it again.

> *Proposition III*
> *The ambiguity of Literature: $\sqrt{-1}$. The*
> *ambiguity of fantasy toward fact, of the*
> *imaginary toward power. And if Imagination*
> *takes Power? And if fact and fantasy some*
> *day converge in the same mental event?*

The aesthetic avant-garde—affinity for the Negative—and the political or ethical avant-garde—desire for the Positive—have not always been distinct. They have come together, sometimes egregiously, in Christian, Romantic, Marxist, and also Fascist art. This last alliance can be grisly. Yet we should not permit the genuine specter of Fascism to inhibit our curiosity about old and new convergences in culture. Can the solitude of the imagination ever be overcome?

What is Art? The text is notorious. A live religious perception of Christian brotherhood must quicken the future of art, so argues Count Leo Tolstoy; for great art always unites, always embraces. "The task of art is enormous. Through the influence of real art, aided by science, guided by religion, that peaceful co-operation of man which is now maintained by external means—by our law-courts, police, charitable institutions, factory inspection, and so forth—should be obtained by man's free and joyous activity." This is the measure of Tolstoy's optimism, for which he was willing to sacrifice *King Lear* and *Anna Karenina.*

Christianity collapsed in Russia before the power of another hope; the optimism of Leon Trotsky was not materially different from that of Tolstoy, the Czarist aristocrat. Proletarian art may be only transitional, Trotsky supposes in *Literature and Revolution,* its sole aim to grasp the historic meaning of change. He notes that Communist and Futurist, politician and artist, are often incompatible in the real world; he does not despair of changing that world. "The wall will fall not only between art and industry," he writes, "but simultaneously between art and nature also." And again: "Social construction and psycho-physical self-education will become two aspects of one and the same process. All the arts—literature, drama, painting, music and architecture will lend this process beautiful form."

Half a century later, with a revolution completed and few walls fallen down, Aleksandr Solzhenitsyn once again takes up the theme of brotherhood under the aegis of art. In *The Nobel Lecture on Literature,* he begins by pondering an enigmatic phrase, not of Tolstoy but of Dostoyevsky: "Beauty will save the world." Solzhenitsyn concludes that a world literature—"a certain common body and common spirit, a living unity of the heart, in which the growing spiritual unity of humanity was expressed"—does indeed exist despite violence, deception, and division. "Writers and artists have a greater opportunity: TO CONQUER THE LIE! In battle with the lie, art has always been victorious, always wins out, visibly, incontrovertibly for all!"

The arguments shift; the rhetoric strains with religious piety, utopian fervor, or humanitarian grandiloquence; but the ancient insistence of the imagination to enter, shape, redeem reality will not be stilled. Nor is this insistence an obsession of the Russian mind alone, of Slavic messianism. The French radical students who now denounce art, artists, and *la vie bohême* do so because these have failed their promise: to alter life as Rimbaud and the Surrealists demanded. Art serves the establishment, serves things as they are, these radicals shout, and their shout finds an echo in Tokyo, Berlin, New York. Posters transform Che Guevara into a pop object of consumption, like Brigitte Bardot; Picasso's "Guernica" does not halt wars but hangs among the masterpieces in the Museum of Modern Art. In the conditions of its production, barter, and ownership, in its assumptions about its uniqueness and value, the art work is a thing of the past, implicated in a bourgeois order which the students themselves, recognizing their own implications in that same order, wish to subvert, wish to transcend.

Note: See *Art and Confrontation* (Greenwich, Conn.: New York Graphic Society, 1968).

Thus it seems that the ambiguity of literature must persist so long as the relation of fiction to fact remains ambiguous, so long as men dream without knowing the limits of their dreams. But the question is also historical. In *Power and Consciousness*, Conor Cruise O'Brien suggests that political theorists seldom hold supreme power: "In these conditions, attention to politics is informed by a wish, a kind of yearning, which makes it preternaturally acute at certain points, perversely obtuse at others. The wish of the political exile takes written form as theory: that is, in Yeats's words, 'grows in pure mind.' The result might be termed *vision-hypothesis:* partaking of the Character of the activity of the poet and prophet, on the one hand, and of the scientist on the other."

In the end, the ambiguity of literature may derive from some deeper, incalculable source: biology, the unconscious, the structure of human needs which guides even the sovereign imagination and determines the conditions under which both fact and fiction are perceived. All change remains within that frame until the frame itself is changed. Even Marxists acknowledge that. Trotsky put it thus: "To reshape the world of feelings, which one has absorbed from one's childhood, by means of a scientific program, is the most difficult inner labor. Not everyone is capable of it. That is why there are many people in this world who think as revolutionists and who feel as Philistines." O'Brien, sensing the common origin of politics and poetry, put it more succinctly: "Yeats's rag-and-bone shop [of the heart] contains a till; Marx's till is situated in a rag-and-bone shop." The issue rests in indeterminacy. Unless:

> *Proposition IV*
> *Dream itself, house of our ancient needs, can*
> *dream a new Imagination of change; unless*
> *Myth becomes also true metamorphosis.*

V. MYTH AND METAMORPHOSIS

Some find in the ambiguity of literature, taken in its classic sense, refuge from change; others turn to more tendentious forms of literature, including ideologies, utopias, fantasies, to quicken or control their ideas of change. Yet these latter forms are themselves embedded in myth:

> In all critical moments of man's social life, the rational forces that resist the rise of the old mythical conceptions are no longer sure of themselves. In these moments the time of myth has come again. For myth has not been really vanquished and sub-

jugated. It is always there, lurking in the dark and
waiting for its hour and opportunity.
Ernst Cassirer, *The Myth of the State*

We think of myth usually as a conservative force. It helps to
create and maintain human consciousness in a hostile universe; it
describes structures of belief which ritual reenacts. This is the back-
ward-looking aspect of myth, turned toward its origins, in *illo tempore*
(Eliade).

But there is another aspect of myth: transformation, from dying
to rising god, from seed to fruit, from fall to spring and back, Osiris
and all the divinities who testify that death itself is only metamorphosis. At first, this seems an action of repetition, of eternal recurrence.
Yet as various mythologues have argued, incarnation, immolation,
and resurrection need not be considered identical events. The relation between the conscious and unconscious mind shifts throughout
the cycles of gods and men. Symbols suffer a sea change. The unconscious itself may prove teleological, Erich Neumann suggests,
working toward a "centroversion" of mind. Or lending itself, as
Cassirer observes, to technological manipulation, creating "synthetic"
myths:

> The new political myths do not grow up freely; they
> are not wild fruits of an exuberant imagination.
> They are artificial things fabricated by very skilful
> and cunning artisans. It has been reserved for the
> twentieth century, our own great technical age, to
> develop a new technique of myth. Henceforth myths
> can be manufactured in the same sense and ac-
> cording to the same methods as any other modern
> weapon—as machine guns or airplanes. That is a
> new thing—and a thing of crucial importance. It
> has changed the whole form of our social life.
> Now the modern political myths proceeded in quite
> a different manner. They did not begin with de-
> manding or prohibiting certain actions. They under-
> took to change the men, in order to be able to
> regulate and control their deeds. The political
> myths acted in the same way as a serpent that
> tries to paralyze its victims before attacking them.
> Men fell victims to them without any serious resis-
> tance.

Myth, then, does not simply stand for the *Urdumheit* of the race.
It slants both backwards and forwards; and in its depths, paradisal and
utopian forms are cognate. Specifically, the myths that empower

contemporary ideologies, utopias, and science fictions in America are not only "myths of concern," as Northrop Frye put it, but also metamorphic myths, structures of change and even of redemption. In short, they imply, as Frye himself recognizes of utopian literature, a theory of education, a notion of *change*.

The mythology of concern, taken as a whole, is not a unified body of knowledge, nor is the knowledge it contains always logically deduced from its beliefs and assumptions, nor does one necessarily believe in everything that one accepts from it. But it does possess a unity nonetheless, and those who have most effectively changed the modern world—Rousseau, Marx, and Freud . . . —are those who have changed the general pattern of our mythology.

The force that creates the myth of concern drives it onward from the specific society one is in to larger and larger groups, and finally toward assimilating the whole of its dialectic. . . . If this were the whole story, the myth of concern would end simply in a vague and fuzzy humanitarianism. But in proportion as one's loyalty stretches beyond one's nation to the whole of the human race, one's concrete and specific human relationships become more obvious.

Northrop Frye, *The Stubborn Structure*

Ideologies, utopias, and fantasies in contemporary America are, at bottom, metamorphic and concerned myths. As such, they are hardly without precedent. In their apocalyptic extreme, such myths express change, Norman Cohn says in *The Pursuit of the Millennium*, "as an event of unique importance, different in kind from all other struggles known to history, a cataclysm from which the world is to emerge totally transformed and redeemed." But the recurrence of this conception does not devalue apocalyptic expectation, which Amos Wilder describes as a certain nakedness to existence, a certain responsiveness "to the unmediated dynamics that underlie all Being and Becoming." Nor should we exaggerate the apocalyptic element in contemporary myths. Very often, that element conveys the sense not of endings but of discontinuities; it resists closure; and it organizes the energy of denial in both spiteful and creative ways. Indeed, the shared power of these metamorphic myths simply draws on a vision of an ideal human condition, deriving from Beginnings and Ends, and in its essentials surprisingly constant.

> *Proposition V*
> *Beginnings and Ends are images of something*
> *vital in the human condition, vital yet virtual,*
> *latent in the present. They are imaginative*

constructs, models not only of private desire
but of human potential.

The question then becomes: Can we classify these models of the human potential, discriminate between them? A simple scheme suggests itself. These models, we may argue, lie between the poles of "objective Fact" and "subjective Fantasy." In between, moving from the former to the latter, we identify the following genres: Futurology, Ideology, Utopian Literature, Science Fiction, Visionary Poetry. Toward one pole, criticism of things as they are prevails; toward the other, synthesis of things as they can be obtains.

A tidy scheme, false and tidy. Even in earlier and less complex epochs, "everyday experience has operated with magical systems of explanation," Karl Mannheim writes in *Ideology and Utopia*. Furthermore, the distinctions between such genres are seldom secure: "It is always the dominant group which is in full accord with the existing order that determines what is to be regarded as utopian, while the ascendant group which is in conflict with things as they are is the one that determines what is regarded as ideological," Mannheim continues. Indeed, the question of truth and artifice precedes that of modern ideologies and utopias. As Harry Levin put it, in *The Myth of the Golden Age in the Renaissance:* "The Occident has lived with two mythologies side by side, one supporting its theological and ethical commitments, the other providing models and conventions for the arts. Traditionally, a sharp line has been drawn between the one and the other, between Christian verity and pagan fiction. But the parallels are strong and the contacts are numerous."

In our own Orwellian world, "simple fact" and "obvious fantasy" almost defy discrimination; they seem to impinge on our consciousness as a single phenomenon.

> In its opening stages, the Watergate affair has shaped up as a very special kind of political struggle. So far, it has not become a clash either of parties or of ideas. Rather, it has been a clash of facts. Recollection has been pitted against recollection, document against document. In the years leading up to Watergate, the country had come to live in a world of Presidential facts. The facts-according-to-the-President . . . had succeeded, that is, in overriding what used to be known as "the facts."
> "Talk of the Town,"
> *The New Yorker*, June 2, 1973

The Orwellian world depends on deception, concealment; its entropic language is the Lie, which Carlyle called "no-thing." But our difficulties, great as they may be with government by mendacity, are not simply political. "Society itself," Daniel Bell says, "becomes a web of consciousness, a form of imagination to be realized as a social construction." This leads to epistemological quandaries. Few thinkers nowadays would blithely maintain that History is descriptive, Fiction constitutive. Pop realism, happenings, the non-fiction novel, the new journalism, the newer technology, no less than Watergate or Madison Avenue, blur our old serviceable sense of fact. The challenge goes back to Nietzsche: "What can be thought must certainly be a fiction." And goes further back to Plato.

The interprenetration of genres, those models of the human potential ranging from futurology to visionary poetry, may be further expected in an age that abhors intellectual purity. Everything has become relevant—why clamor for relevance?—and nothing extraneous. Few contemporary models of change are based on "closed myths," containing their own answer and forming, as Frye says, "a body of major premises which is superior in authority to scholarship and art." The development of Marxism into its various mutants is to the point.

> "The graffiti of the '*jeunesse en colère*' joined Karl Marx and André Breton; the slogan '*l'imagination au pouvoir*' went well with '*les comités partout*'; the piano with the jazz player stood well between the barricades. . . ."
> Jean-Paul Sartre?
>
> "Utopian possibilities are inherent in the technical and technological forces of advanced capitalism and socialism: the rational utilization of these forces on a global scale would terminate poverty and scarcity within a foreseeable future."
> Buckminster Fuller?
>
> ". . . incompatible with any society governed by the Profit and Performance Principle . . . [the revolution] would mean the ascent of the Aesthetic Principle as Form of the Reality Principle. . . ."
> Echoes of Norman O. Brown?
>
> In fact, Herbert Marcuse, *An Essay on Liberation*, pp. 22, 4, 90.

The question, then, still stands: how to classify these models of the human potential, how to discriminate between types of change? Without a theory of change, without a consensus of values, without divine revelation, it is doubtful that any answer will possess permanence or authority. There are structural definitions to which we may agree. Each model specifies its own mythic or dramatic form, its epiphany of peripety. Each projects its theogony or heroic parentage, its theomachy or human agon. Each expresses its particular sense of time or duration, its peculiar cosmology or earthly sense of space. In short, we can agree to view these models as verbal constructs whose content may be irrelevant to our definition, whose truth and value are mainly configurational. Having done so, we may suddenly discover that all vital and vexing questions remain unanswered within our structuralist frames.

Structures, shallow or deep, may constrain our languages and even our actions. Yet Chomsky himself states in *Problems of Knowledge and Freedom:* "Knowledge of language results from the interplay of initially given structures of mind, maturational processes, and interaction with the environment. Thus there is no reason to expect that there will be invariant properties of the knowledge that is acquired—the grammars constructed by the mind—even if the innate determination of initial structures and maturational processes is quite restrictive." The grammars of the mind include models of change, and the best of these are forms of creation, creating values before they come to be valued.

Let classifications come later if they must.

VI. NOTES ON SOME MODELS OF CHANGE

Models of change, based on various metamorphic and redemptive myths, abound in contemporary American culture. Whatever else they may be, these models are verbal structures. However obliquely, such structures also are, as Jacques Derrida observes in *L'Écriture et la différence*, teleological: their ends are made present throughout their forms. All imply an ideology.

The choice and sequence of five models which I present on these pages also express, no doubt, a silent ideology on my part. I confess to it candidly, and would further add: I like the first models far less than the last. My commentary makes no attempt to disguise preference or, I hope, to ignore fact. Yet in the end it is a matter of tact.

A. Herman Kahn

Futurology thrives. Its devotees range from scientists of the RAND Corporation to science fiction writers, from militarists to occultists. Isaac Asimov, Daniel Bell, Gaston Berger, I. Bestuzher-Lada, Kenneth Boulding, John Cage, Arthur C. Clarke, Bertrand de Jouvenel, C. A. Doxiadis, Gerald Feinberg, R. Buckminster Fuller, Dennis Gabor, Yujiro Hayashi, Olaf Helmer, Erich Jantsch, Robert Jungk, Herman Kahn, John McHale, Marshall McLuhan, Margaret Mead, Donella H. and Dennis L. Meadows, Aurelio Peccei, Fred L. Polak, Alvin Toffler, Anthony Wiener, alphabetically but in their sundry ways, dedicate themselves to things to come. Institutes for the study of the future fill our space, and periodicals like *The Futurist, Futures, Changes* extend our time. The "scenario" has become the thing.

> *Note:* Departments of literature, please ponder: here lies a new field. How will the verbal imagination sow its seed? For bibliographic aid, see John Brockman and Edward Rosenfeld, eds., *Real Time 1* (Garden City, N.Y.: Doubleday, 1973); Alvin Toffler, ed., *The Futurists* (New York: Random House, 1972); and Michael Marien, ed., *The Hot List Delphi* (Syracuse, N.Y.: Syracuse University Research Corporation, 1972).

Among American futurologists, Herman Kahn seems to relish his role notoriously. Like Daniel Bell, Kahn basks in the warmth of the Establishment, and hails the evolution of a world-wide "post-industrial" society, governed rationally by a "responsible center," resistant to the values of the "far Right" as well as "the humanist Left." (Oh, these men do not prophesy: from the heart of a meritocratic society, they clearly project.) The director of the Hudson Institute will admit that such visions as Wells's, Huxley's, and Orwell's may have greater impact on society than systematic studies of the future. As an expert, however, Kahn distinguishes between "projection," extrapolation into the future; "forecast," which assigns a rough order of probability to various events; and "prediction," establishing overwhelming probability in favor of a specific event. Thus Kahn projects The Basic, Long-Term Multifold Trend toward:

1. Increasingly Sensate (empirical, this-worldly, secular, humanistic, pragmatic, utilitarian, contractual, epicurean or hedonistic, and the like) cultures
2. Bourgeois, bureaucratic, "meritocratic," democratic (and nationalistic?) elites
3. Accumulation of scientific and technological knowledge
4. Institutionalization of change, especially re-

search, development, innovation, and diffusion
5. Worldwide industrialization and modernization
6. Increasing affluence and (recently) leisure
7. Population growth
8. Urbanization and (soon) the growth of megalopolises
9. Decreasing importance of primary and (recently) secondary occupations
10. Literacy and education
11. Increasing capability for mass destruction
12. Increasing tempo of change
13. Increasing universality of the multifold trend

Herman Kahn and Anthony Wiener,
The Year 2000 (1967)

In a later work co-authored with B. Bruce-Briggs, *Things to Come* (1972), Kahn modifies this list slightly, adding two points: increasing centralization of economic and political power, increasing use of manipulative social engineering. (Here Kahn and Skinner meet.) So much for the "surprise-free" Multifold Trend.

One wonders: do we need the Hudson Institute to confirm the obvious? Perhaps. A "surprise-free" projection, after all, is one that brings no surprises to its author. Yet Kahn knows enough to add: "The most surprising thing that can happen in a broad, long-range, surprise-free projection is that there will be no surprises." What, then, does this model of change lack?

Although Kahn sees the difference between "descriptive" and "normative" futurology, his models actually blur that difference; they are not "value-free." His scenario is not only a "hypothetical sequence of events" but also a crypto-plan to fulfill certain events.

Kahn believes himself to be writing from the center of reality, in the mainstream of "macro-history." He can be vivid in discerning certain large patterns. But his sense of creativity, of contingency in human affairs, never threatens his perceived position within history. His assumption is this: the trends set forth by the industrial revolution have "a staying power" which, despite various setbacks, enables extrapolation. Conveniently, the trends that have "staying power" are those he approves.

Extrapolation also works for him backwards. Kahn warns futurologists against historical analogies but revels in them himself. New ideologies prove to be only variations of the old: "neo-anarchism," "neo-syndicalism," "neo-fascism." Similarly, new philosophies and attitudes are called: "neo-epicurean," "neo-stoic," "neo-gentleman." The world is moving into a new Hellenistic age, termed "Westernistic," "expanding its material horizons but lacking in spiritual content." Kahn sees no reason to malign that age: it may last seven hundred years!

An optimist, a Pelagian, an anti-Malthusian (like Fuller), Kahn reveals a certain flamboyance of hope. He affronts the pieties of academe. This may be admirable. But his affronts avoid intellectual subtlety. For instance: "(Even a severe backlash against the intellectuals would probably, to a large degree, be led by intellectuals—e.g., Hitler, Goebbels, Kaltenbrunner, et al.) The intellectuals have a great effect on society. They indirectly mold public opinion." Where values are concerned, where the intricacies of feeling and desire come into play, where anything like a human *destiny* is at stake, Kahn betrays a stubborn smallness of mind.

Sponsored by various government agencies and multinational corporations, the Hudson Institute projects models of a society that wants to become more: more of what it already is. It is a society shaped by its senses, demanding satisfactions both fine and crude.

B. B. F. Skinner

Behaviorism also appeals to the senses only, but it is messianic, messianically crude. Here the concept of man is one of surfaces, for surfaces are what we can observe and so control.

> Autonomous man is a device used to explain what we cannot explain in any other way. He has been constructed from our ignorance, and as our understanding increases, the very stuff of which he is comprised vanishes.
>
> Freedom is a matter of contingencies of reinforcement. . . .
>
> We must look to the contingencies that induce people to act to increase the chances that their cultures will survive.
>
> The evolution of a culture is a gigantic exercise in self-control. . . . We have not yet seen what man can make of man.
>
> B. F. Skinner,
> *Beyond Freedom and Dignity* (1971)

Skinner's model assumes consent to a technology of behavior. Ignoring inner processes of mind, Skinner wants to remake human and animal behavior by a process of "positive reinforcements," controls.

Pigeons can be taught to walk tracing the figure 8; men can be taught not to be good but to act well. There is a certain simplicity in this, a certain appeal; and the appeal becomes almost seductive in Skinner's utopian novel, *Walden Two*.

No need to compare the minds behind Waldens One and Two. Skinner is a distinguished scientist; let his peers judge him there. But we are all called to judge the reformer, the new-former of men. Does he require imagination? Skinner conceals its evidence too well. He seems an innocent about the human race, what we have been, are, and must become. Consider, for instance, the sexual element in *Walden Two:* benign certainly and prophylactic. Yet can such feeble "free affection" break the ancient bonds of Eros and Thanatos?

Still, Skinner's model contains an educational theory: behavioral engineering. We know it also by its old name: torture. Behavioral engineering, torture, rehabilitation: these are all names for our Modern Mystery Play. Aldous Huxley saw the point. On revisiting his Brave New World, chillingly he noted that the Grand Inquisitor now commands more than "miracle, mystery, and authority"; he possesses new technologies to enact them. But let us grant Skinner the premise of a benevolent technology: not torture, an educational theory. About the politics of that theory, about its ethics or aesthetics, about its languages, about its goals, Skinner offers tautologies, banalities. All his demands point to a retreat from consciousness. Yet consciousness in our world does not retreat: it expands.

Skinner has a certain courage, the courage to become. Curiously, his statements seem like a dead echo of "Whosoever shall lose his life shall find it. . . ." But what paltry thing does Skinner mean by "life"?

C. Herbert Marcuse

From Marx to Mao, from Ho to Che, the earth labors to revive in blood a socialist dream.

Marcuse, thrusting the twentieth century upon Marx, creates a model of change which seems elusively familiar. Critical, historical, its utopian tilt now vanishes and now spins into view. Some of Marcuse's early works are opaque and glum. Their ideas are restrained by the rationalities not of history but of orthodoxy. Yet their central perception still breaks through, exposing our consciousness to our politics. Flattened into the administered plane of the "Welfare-Warfare state," Marcuse argues, man seeks to recover his "negativity," his powers of criticism and transcendence; for even Eros has become a victim of reactionary "desublimation"; and even "repressive tolerance" has turned into an agent of control.

> However, underneath the conservative popular base is the substratum of the outcasts and outsiders, the exploited and persecuted of other races and other colors, the unemployed and the unemployable. . . . Thus their opposition is revolutionary even if their consciousness is not.
>
> Herbert Marcuse,
> *One-Dimensional Man* (1964)

Marcuse admits that critical theory is weakest in its "inability to demonstrate the liberating tendencies *within* the established society." Thus we remain caught in the vicious circle of "determinate negation"; we are never certain how things do become other than what they are. Yet in his later works, Marcuse opens himself to new utopian possibilities; he seeks new pressure points of change. The cultural revolution, the alteration of consciousness, the structure of human needs, even the power of dreams, enter his field of political vision. Remarkably, Marcuse moves closer to Breton, to Artaud, even to Brown.

> This qualitative change must occur in the needs, in the infrastructure of man. . . . Such a change would constitute the instinctual basis for freedom which the long history of class society has blocked.

> . . . radical social change will involve a radical transformation of nature. Also of the *science* of nature? Nature as manifestation of subjectivity: the idea seems inseparable from teleology—long since taboo in Western science. Nature as object per se fitted all too well into the universe of the capitalist treatment of matter to allow discarding the taboo.

> Technique would then tend to become art, and art would tend to form reality: the opposition between imagination and reason, higher and lower faculties, poetic and scientific thought, would be invalidated.
>
> Herbert Marcuse,
> *An Essay on Liberation* (1969)

> If art dreams of liberation within the spectrum of history, dream realization through revolution must be possible—the surrealist program must be still valid.
>
> Herbert Marcuse,
> *Counterrevolution and Revolt* (1972)

Astonishing Marxist! Yet this freedom of thought, this play of "historical Reason," is also weighted. Sometimes the style betrays Marcuse, sometimes it is the very structure of Western philosophy. For him, as for Hegel and Marx, "Reason *per se*" continues to speak, through "objective" reality, in its ancient cadences. The rest is mysticism, mystification; the rest is unpolitical. Contrariwise: "The most extreme political content does not repel traditional forms" in art, Marcuse believes; he has little patience with anti-art.

What then does Marcuse lack? Perhaps true anticipatory force. His categories seem always to lag behind cultural realities—except in *Eros and Civilization* (1955)? Erudition, critical energy, high moral earnestness, surprising ability to adapt to time: yes. But prophecy? Perhaps no political imagination can ever be prophetic.

> *Note:* In their controversy (*Commentary*, February and March, 1967), Brown replies to Marcuse: "Reason is power; powerful arguments; power-politics; *Realpolitik;* reality-principle. Love comes emptyhanded; the eternal proletariat; like Cordelia, bringing No-thing."

D. R. Buckminster Fuller

He begins with a conclusion: "Universe is not a failure." All the rest follows.

Architect (unlicensed), inventor (Geodesic dome, Dymaxion house and car, Computerized World game), cartographer (Dymaxion map), mathematician (some say trivial, some hail the Octet Truss, others enjoy $\frac{n^2 - n}{2}$: "universe is plural and at minimum—two"), cosmologist ("Nature is not only orderly but the orderliness is rationally accountable in pure principle. . . . Understanding is symmetrically tetrahedronal"), poet (or at least author of visionary "ventilated prose"), and prophet (*Utopia or Oblivion*), Fuller appears, above all, as a Generalist, a student of Whole Systems, a Comprehensive Design Scientist.

He begins with a conviction, and like his Transcendentalist forebears—inverse Puritans though Puritans still—he ends with a determination: to make man "a success in Universe." Regeneration is one of his favored concepts. Regeneration not of souls but of systems, of environments. How?

Nature abhors irrationality, nor does it use π. The Coordinate System of Universe is "omnirational"; it responds to human intelligence, as if in love. Within that Coordinate System, the mind acts to fulfill its function, its destiny. Consider this triangle of ideas (the basic, stable relationship in the universe is triangular, Fuller insists):

Synergy

Universe, by definition, and its derivative concepts are *synergetic. Synergy* . . . means *unique behav-*

Ephemeralization

Doing vastly more with vastly and invisibly less is known technically as *ephemeralization.* The mass produc-

iors of whole systems unpredicted by
any behaviors of their component
functions taken separately.

tion of electronic controls inaugurated
automation. With automation has
come—just now—a dawning awareness of the *invisible avalanche of
ephemeralization.*

Antientropy or Syntropy

Man is the great antientropy of universe. The famous "Second Law" of Thermodynamics propounds
entropy. But the human mind discovered and described and harnessed in orderly fashion this dis-
orderly propensity of nature. Einstein's mind discovered and generalized the comprehensive law of
physical energy universe as $E = mc^2$ and the *process* of metaphysical mastery of the physical is ir-
reversible.

R. Buckminster Fuller, *Utopia or Oblivion* (1969)

A synergetic universe, a technology that enables us increasingly
to do more with less, meta-physical regeneration through mind: these
are cornerstones in Fuller's triadic model. Newton and Malthus are
refuted; neither rest nor scarcity will prevail. We only have to "hook
into the universe's comprehensive evolutionary system—for the universe
is the minimum and only perpetual-motion machine." We "hook into"
it through a "design revolution." It is a grand vision of change, weakest
in its excesses of rationality.

At times, Fuller seems to address another species, not our perverse
own. His naïve numbers, his very prophecies, miss the mark. He
revives not only Emerson at his best but also Rousseau at his worst.
Someone once said of Fuller: "He does not see negatives." Indeed,
some positives are invisible to him as well. And his Pythagorean sym-
metries, turning technological, sometimes turn bland or leave the
mind blank.

> *Note:* Hugh Kenner's study *Bucky* (1973) gives a crackling
> "Dialogue with a Skeptic," which summons all the best argu-
> ments for advocate and skeptic alike.

Yet as Fuller himself states: "I never argue." This is not egoism
but faith in the true order of things. Such faith can liberate odd
perceptions in all their original force. Quite at random, twelve points
to celebrate Fuller's twelve-point vector equilibrium (the old cu-
boctahedron):

- Geodesics and viruses reveal cognate structures
- Wealth is energy multiplied by knowhow

- Politics means war, and either war is obsolete or we are
- Continuous Man, the sum of all consciousness, can only grow
- General principles may be bouncing around weightlessly in the universe
- Vertical, against gravity, is the dimension of life
- Automation ends specialization
- All actions are the product of qualities inherent in nature
- Telepathy may be electro-magnetic
- Motion in the universe is still a mystery
- Humanity possesses an innate teleological sense of general principles
- The manifest destiny of Spaceship Earth is syntropic

More than any of our model-makers, R. Buckminister Fuller gives man a spacious role in the cosmos. Yet he does not rule out "oblivion"; at seventy-three, he was ready to admit that "residual ignorance," "shortsightedness," and "circumstance-biased viewpoints" may carry humanity beyond the "point of no return." Above all, Fuller, the comprehensive rationalist, does not rule out mystery:

> Humans grope for *absolute* understanding,
> Unmindful of the a priori mystery
> Which inherently precludes
> *Absolute* understanding
> R. Buckminster Fuller,
> *Intuition* (1972)

E. *Norman O. Brown*

This leads to Brown.

We can be brief.

The last line of *Love's Body*:

"Everything is only metaphor; there is only poetry."

Symbolism.

Marcuse chides Brown: "Unless the analysis takes the road of return from the symbolic to the literal, from the illusion to the reality of the illusion, it remains ideological, replacing one mystification with another." But re-turn to what? Brown goes beyond the conventional terms of symbolism: reality and illusion are not only reversed, everything is also real and everything illusory. Perhaps that is mystification. Or is it rather the premise for the transformation of existence, its transfiguration? Change is vision, light on the body, consciousness in the dark becoming new light.

Brown demands loss of Self, abolition of the Reality Principle, Resurrection of the Body, knowledge of Nothing. History, philosophy, anthropology, psychoanalysis offer metaphors to his poetry. Let us simply say that in his writings all the sacred and profane thoughts of mankind conspire alchemically to re-create the soul:

The real birth would be birth from the womb of the dream world   The real death is the death we are dead with here and now   To heal is to make whole, as in whole-some; to make one again; to unify or reunify: this is Eros in action   There is only one political problem in our world today: the unification of mankind   The solution of the problem of identity is get lost   In orgasm, all the splendor and misery of representative government. The representative organ acts on behalf of the entire organism   The shape of the body awake, the shape of the resurrected body, is not vertical but perverse and polymorphous; not a straight line but a circle   Upside down   Not the reality-principle but surrealism   The mad truth: the boundary between sanity and insanity is a false one   Intellect is sacrifice of intellect, or fire; which burns up as it gives light   To let the silence in is symbolism   Symbolism is polymorphous perversity   Speech resexualized   The sper-matic word, the word as seed   Admit the void   The virgin womb of the imagination in which the word be-comes flesh is silence   Norman O. Brown, Love's Body (1966)

The model is coherent. In a sense, Brown is the major restatement of Blake in our century—and possibly of Calvin! Brown: "Man makes Himself, his own body, in the symbolic freedom of the imagination. . . . The body is plastic; the imagination esemplastic." In dreams begin the responsibilities of men to become gods. The process, again, is poetry. "The permanent revolution, the perpetual reformation, is vision, is spontaneity, perpetually renewed. . . ."

Here is a truly radical vision. And truly reactionary. For *there is no change*, as we understand it, in the universe of Brown. The universe is already *given*. Its innermost principle is obedience, a Calvinist obedience to the whole. Here is anthropophany: "The real atheism is to become divine. In a dialectical view, atheism becomes theurgy, godmaking; demystification becomes the discovery of a new mystery; and everything remains the same." Is there finally any Grace? The way forward is always back. *Closing Time* (1973):

> "back
> back to the original goat-song"

But "back" simply means:

> "The origin of language in fantasy,
> not in reality"

* * *

Epiphanies leave a certain deadness in the air. We wonder: has anything really changed? Here we stand, as always, between the womb and rotting grave. Here we stand.

Change may be our ultimate fiction. But fiction may also be our ultimate persuasion to change. In a sense, all true prophecies are self-fulfilling prophecies: they help to transform mystery into history. In that sense, the foregoing models of transformation act on self or environment, on consciousness or nature, sometimes equating both. In doing so, they seek an Archimedean point:

For Kahn: The Sensate Process
For Skinner: Behavioral Engineering
For Marcuse: Reason and Political Revolution
For Fuller: Regeneration through Comprehensive Design
For Brown: From Metaphor to Revelation

The rubrics shift: from matter to mind, mind in which matter is wholly reconciled. Ideology, utopia, fantasy—and even science—all meeting? In Atlantis?

VII. AMERICA AND ATLANTIS

Wherever Atlantis may have been or will be, some say that the energy of American illusion helps to discover it—and to corrupt it. Gatsby's "incomparable milk of wonder"—and "foul dust that trails his dreams." Springing from some flawed Platonic concept of ourselves, we still perpetuate the doubleness of the Dream. It is an ancient story. The land bridge, during the Pleistocene, linked Asia and America: huge shaggy animals, our totem fathers, lumbered into the new world. The land bridge dissolved into the sea and millennial years. What memories did these great beasts—the bison, the bear, the elk, the mammoth, and the great sloth—retain of an undivided earth? Men and women somehow appeared. Indian and Viking, Spaniard and Puritan, lived their own gentle or bloody myths on the land. But how did these human creatures sleep in America, and of what did they dream? Their descendants thrust themselves against inner and outer frontiers. "Thus are our first steps trod, thus are our first trees felled, in general, by the most vicious of our people," St. Jean de Crèvecoeur wrote—adding about his fellow immigrants: "He no sooner breathes our air than he forms schemes, and embarks in designs he never would have thought of in his own country." The Republic dedicated itself to the pursuit of happiness, rejecting "the history of the world," which, as Hegel was to say, "is not the theatre of happiness." But America also made greedy, deadly history. It invaded the twentieth century, grasped the moon. Atlantis recedes; America grows. Yet within the moist, dark imagination, men and women still seek alternative realities to plastic plains and cities of steel. They seek, beyond "struggling afflictions," Blake's prophecy of America: "another portion of the infinite." It is not a place: there is an informing power of the mind that neither "Atlantis" nor "America" circumscribes. It is all together human and more than human.

Index

Böll, Heinrich, 112
Borges, Jorge Luis, 44, 83, 86, 90, 93,
    111, 140, 141; *Ficciones,* 86
Boulding, Kenneth, 166
Bradbury, Ray, 112, 113
Brand, Stewart, 153; *The Whole
    Earth Catalog* (ed.), 57, 103
Brautigan, Richard, 83, 107–108; *In
    Watermelon Sugar,* 108; *Trout
    Fishing in America,* 108
Brecht, Bertolt, 44, 155
Brel, Jacques, 17
Breton, André, 56, 164, 170
Brockman, John, 107, 123, 166;
    Afterwords, 123; *By the Late John
    Brockman,* 107; *Real Time 1* (ed.),
    166
Bronowski, Jacob, 125
Brooks, Van Wyck, 44, 101
Brown, Cecil, *The Life and Loves of
    Mr. Jiveass Nigger,* 103
Brown, Norman O., 14, 16n, 17, 25,
    46, 55, 56, 65, 66, 79, 80, 88, 102,
    122, 132, 144, 147n, 164, 170, 171,
    173–175; *Closing Time,* 79n, 175;
    Love's Body, 122, 147n, 173, 174
Bruce-Biggs, B., *Things to Come,* 167
Bruno, Giordano, 63, 91, 139
Brzezinsky, Zbigniew, *Between Two
    Ages: America's Role in the
    Technetronic Era,* 124–125
Buber, Martin, 5, 15n, 102; *Between
    Man and Man,* 15n
Budgen, Frank, 83, 89
Burgess, Anthony, 70, 83, 142
Burke, Kenneth, 10
Burroughs, William, 8, 12, 24, 44, 57,
    69, 83, 93, 101, 111, 114, 140–141,
    142; *Naked Lunch,* 140; *The Soft
    Machine,* 12; *The Ticket That Ex-
    ploded,* 140
Butor, Michel, 44, 56, 79, 80, 83, 86,
    87, 140

Cage, John, 21–22, 23, 46, 53–54, 87,
    102, 109, 112, 138, 166; *A Year
    from Monday,* 23, 138
Calvin, John, 175
Campbell, Joseph, 133
Camus, Albert, 7, 8, 9, 15n, 21, 33,
    155; *The Myth of Sisyphus,* 15n;
    Resistance, Rebellion, and Death,
    15n
Capote, Truman, 56, 86, 100; *In Cold
    Blood,* 86
Carlyle, Thomas, 107, 164
Carroll, Lewis, 89

Cassirer, Ernst, 8, 160–161; *The Myth
    of the State,* 160–161
Castaneda, Carlos, 55, 56
Cather, Willa, 100
Céline, Louis Ferdinand, 69
Cervantes, Miguel de, *Don Quixote,* 8
Char, René, 12
Chomsky, Noam, 132, 165; *Problems
    of Knowledge and Freedom,* 165
Chuang Tse, 144
Cioran, E. M., 55
Cixous, Hélène, 94
Clarke, Arthur, 112, 166; *2001: A
    Space Odyssey,* 127, 133
Claudel, Paul, 155
Cleaver, Eldridge, 102
Coffin, William Sloane, 106
Cohen, Leonard, 17, 115; *The Beauti-
    ful Losers,* 115
Cohen, Marvin, *The Self-Devoted
    Friend,* 107
Cohn, Norman, *The Pursuit of the
    Millennium,* 162
Coleridge, Samuel Taylor, 8
Colum, Mary, 65, 79
Connolly, Cyril, 44
Conrad, Joseph, 41
Cooper, David, 89
Coover, Robert, *The Universal Base-
    ball Association,* 141
Corso, Gregory, 101
Cortazar, Julio, 86, 140; *Hopscotch,*
    86
Crèvecoeur, St. Jean de, 176
Croce, Benedetto, 8
Curtius, Ernst Robert, 79

Daiches, David, 32
Dante Alighieri, 63
Darwin, Charles, 151
Debray, Régis, 102
De Gaulle, Charles, 103
Deleuze, Gilles, xiv
Delgado, José, 92, 136–137
Demby, William, *The Catacombs,* 103
Derrida, Jacques, xiv, 140, 165;
    L'Écriture et la différence, 165
Descartes, René, 72
Döblin, Alfred, 49, 86, 87; *Alexander-
    platz Berlin,* 87
Donleavy, J. P., 109
Dos Passos, John, 49, 87; *U.S.A.,* 87
Dostoyevsky, Fyodor, 159
Doxiadis, C. A., 166
Dubuffet, Jean, xiii
Duchamp, Marcel, 21, 23, 31, 42, 47,
    53, 54, 111

Durrell, Lawrence, 5, 15n; *Art and Outrage*, 15n
Dylan, Bob, 17, 102

Egbert, Donald Drew, *Social Realism and the Arts*, 158
Ehrmann, Jacques, xiv
Einstein, Albert, 125, 151, 172; *Ideas and Opinions*, 125
Eliade, Mircea, 133–134, 161; *Myths, Dreams, and Mysteries*, 133–134
Eliot, T. S., xii, 31, 41, 43, 49, 50, 56, 59, 82, 140, 155; *The Waste Land*, xii, 46
Elkin, Stanley, 101
Ellis, Havelock, 88
Ellison, Ralph, 101
Ellmann, Richard, 48, 64, 72, 84–85; *The Tradition of the Modern* (ed.), 48
Ellul, Jacques, *The Technological Society*, 134
Emerson, Ralph Waldo, 121, 147n, 172; *Nature*, 121, 147n
Empson, William, 44
Esfandiary, F. M., *Optimism One: The Emerging Radicalism*, 125
Euler, Leonhard, 121
Euripides, 42; *The Bacchae*, 39

Fanon, Frantz, 102
Faulkner, William, 8, 31, 41, 49, 56, 86, 100, 155; *The Sound and the Fury*, 80
Federman, Raymond, 87, 141; *Double or Nothing*, 141
Feidelson, Charles, Jr., *The Tradition of the Modern* (ed.), 48
Feinberg, Gerald, 92, 122, 129, 130, 147n, 166; *The Prometheus Project*, 92, 122, 129, 130, 147n
Ferkiss, Victor, *Technological Man*, 125
Ferlinghetti, Lawrence, 101
Fiedler, Leslie, 45, 81, 101, 105; *Collected Essays*, 45; *Waiting for the End*, 105
Flaubert, Gustave, 78
Fletcher, John, 90
Foucault, Michel, xiv, 140
Frank, Joseph, 50, 86; *The Widening Gyre*, 50
Fraser, G. S., 156
Freud, Sigmund, 9, 116–117, 151, 162
Friedman, Bruce Jay, 101
Frohock, W. M., 32

Frye, Northrop, 10, 11–12, 15n, 24, 27, 44, 51, 80, 90, 113, 156, 162, 164; *Anatomy of Criticism*, 10; *The Modern Century*, 51, 156; *The Stubborn Structure*, 162; *The Well-Tempered Critic*, 11–12, 15n
Fuchs, Daniel, 101
Fuller, R. Buckminster, 52, 54, 55, 92, 97, 102, 103, 110, 122, 123, 124, 135–136, 138, 147n, 164, 166, 168, 171–173, 175; *Intuition*, 122, 147n, 173; *Utopia or Oblivion*, 171–172

Gabo, Naum, 50
Gabor, Dennis, 152, 166
Galilei, Galileo, 116
Gass, William, 109
Genesis, 132
Genet, Jean, 12, 30, 36, 43, 69, 86, 140, 156–157; *Funeral Rites*, 157; *Journal d'un voleur*, 86
Gide, André, 41, 85–86, 111, 131, 155; *Les Faux-Monnayeurs (The Counterfeiters)*, 85–86, 111
Gilbert, Stuart, 77
Glascow, Ellen, 100
Glasheen, Adaline, 93
Godwin, Francis, 112
Goebbels, Paul Joseph, 168
Goethe, Johann Wolfgang von, xii, 47, 128, 129, 156; *Dr. Faustus*, 50; *Prometheus: A Dramatic Fragment*, 129
Gogarty, Oliver, 78–79
Gold, Herbert, 101
Gombrowicz, Witold, 31, 86; *Ferdydurke*, 86
Goodman, Paul, 57, 102
Gospel of Truth, The, 121, 147n
Goyen, William, 100
Grass, Günter, 41, 155
Grau, Shirley Ann, 100
Graves, Morris, 23
Greene, Graham, 8
Guevara, Che, 159, 169
Gysin, Brion, 12

Haldane, J. B. S., 104
Halperin, Ann, 22
Hassan, Ihab, 31, 32, 33–34, 36, 45, 67; *The Dismemberment of Orpheus*, 29–36, 43, 139; *Liberations* (ed.), 45; *Literature of Silence*, 45, 67
Hawkes, John, 86, 101, 115; *The Cannibal*, 86; *The Lime Twig*, 115

Hayashi, Yujiro, 166
Hegel, Georg Wilhelm Friedrich, 47,
    139, 140, 170, 176
Heidegger, Martin, xiv, 46, 140
Heilbrun, Carolyn, 89
Heinlein, Robert, 112, 142–143;
    Stranger in a Strange Land,
    142–143
Heisenberg, Werner, 103
Heller, Erich, *The Artist's Journey to
    the Interior,* 47, 139
Heller, Joseph, 109
Helmer, Olaf, 166
Hemingway, Ernest, 30, 31, 34, 41,
    43, 59, 102, 155
Hendrix, Jimi, 126–127
Heraclitus, 152
Hesiod, *Theogony, Works and Days,*
    128, 129
Hitler, Adolf, 168
Ho Chi Minh, 169
Hoffman, Frederick, *The Mortal No,*
    19
Holmes, John Clellon, 101
Homer, 66
Howe, Irving, 44
Hoyle, Fred, *The Black Cloud,* 142
Hulme, T. E., 82
Husserl, Edmund, xiv, 56, 140
Huxley, Aldous, 112, 166, 169; *Brave
    New World,* 112

Ibsen, Henrik, 20

Jackson, George, *Soledad Brother,* 157
Jantsch, Erich, 166
Jarry, Alfred, 44, 69, 111; *Ubu Roi,* 44
Jeans, Sir James, 116, 121, 147n; *The
    Mysterious Universe,* 121, 147n
Jesus, 57
Jewett, Sarah Orne, 100
John the Divine, Saint, 14; *Revelation,*
    14, 16n
Johns, Jasper, 24
Johnson, Virginia E., 136
Jolas, Eugene, 81
Jonas, Hans, *The Gnostic Religion,*
    131
Jones, LeRoi. *See* Baraka, Amiri
Jouvenel, Bertrand de, 166
Joyce, James, xi, 8, 13, 15n, 31, 41,
    43, 44, 49, 53, 56, 63–73, 77–94,
    140; *Finnegans Wake,* xi, 13, 31,
    44, 48, 63, 65, 66, 67, 68, 70, 71,
    73, 77–94, 132; *Portrait of the
    Artist as a Young Man,* 80; *Ulysses,*

8–9, 15n, 46; *Work in Progress,*
    68
Joyce, Lucia, 65
Joyce, Nora, 66, 78
Jung, Carl Gustav, 65, 79
Jungk, Robert, 166

Kafka, Franz, 13, 22, 30, 31, 36, 41,
    43, 48, 69, 84, 140; *The Castle
    (Das Schloss),* 49, 80
Kahler, Erich, *The Inward Turn of
    Narrative,* 140
Kahn, Herman, 165, 166–168, 175;
    Things to Come, 167; *The Year
    2000,* 167
Kahn, Louis, 122, 147n
Kaltenbrunner, Ernst, 168
Kant, Immanuel, 8
Kateb, George, 154
Kazin, Alfred, 44
Kelley, William Melvin, 101
Kells, The Book of, 67, 87
Kennedy, John F., 103
Kenner, Hugh, 45, 83, 87, 172; *Bucky,*
    172; *The Counterfeiters,* 45;
    Samuel Beckett, 45; *The Stoic
    Comedians,* 87
Kepler, Johannes, 112, 125
Kerényi, C. K., 129, 131; *Prometheus:
    Archetypal Image of Human
    Existence,* 129
Kermode, Frank, 24, 44, 47, 155;
    Continuities, 47; *The Sense of an
    Ending,* 24
Kerouac, Jack, 101
Kesey, Ken, 56
Khrushchev, Nikita, 103
Kierkegaard, Søren, 9
Kirby, Michael, *The Art of Time,* 58
Klinkowitz, Jerome, *Innovative Fic-
    tion: Stories for the Seventies* (ed.),
    142
Koestler, Arthur, *The Ghost in the
    Machine,* 125; *The Roots of
    Coincidence,* 125n
Kosinski, Jerzy, 23–24, 105–106; *The
    Painted Bird,* 23–24; *Steps,* 23,
    105–106
Kraft-Ebbing, R., 88
Krieger, Murray, 7, 14, 15n, 16n;
    The Tragic Vision, 7, 15n

Laing, R. D., 56
Langbaum, Robert, *The Modern
    Tradition,* 56
Lautréamont, Compte de (Isadore
    Ducasse), 13, 16n, 48, 110

Scholes, Robert, *Learners and Discerners* (ed.), 45
Schorer, Mark, 44
Schwartz, Barry, 135
Schwartz, Delmore, 40–41
Schwarzkogler, Rudolph, 43
Scott, Nathan A., Jr., 33, 51; *The Broken Center*, 51
Seale, Bobby, 155, 157
Selby, Hubert, 57
Senn, Fritz, 88
Sewell, Elizabeth, *The Structure of Poetry*, 67
Shakespeare, William, 88, 135, 156; *Hamlet*, 8; *King Lear*, 158
Shapiro, Karl, 8, 15n, 44; *Beyond Criticism*, 44; *In Defence of Ignorance*, 44; *Start with the Sun*, 8, 15n
Shaw, George Bernard, 79
Shelley, Mary, *Frankenstein: or, The Modern Prometheus*, 129, 130, 131
Shelley, Percy Bysshe, 129, 131, 155; *Prometheus Unbound*, 129
Sherrington, Sir Charles, 104
Sibelius, Jean, 20
Silone, Ignazio, 8
Sinbad the Sailor, 112
Skinner, B. F., 52, 167, 168–169, 175; *Beyond Freedom and Dignity*, 168; *Walden Two*, 169
Slote, Bernice, *Start with the Sun*, 8, 15n
Snow, C. P., 156
Soleri, Paolo, *The Bridge between Matter and Spirit Is Matter Becoming Spirit*, 92
Sollers, Philippe, 22, 56; *Nombres*, 22
Solomon, Margaret, 87, 88
Solzhenitsyn, Aleksandr, xvi, 159; *The Nobel Lecture on Literature*, 159
Somer, John, *Innovative Fiction: Stories for the Seventies* (ed.), 142
Sontag, Susan, 22, 45, 58, 93; *Against Interpretation*, 45; *Styles of Radical Will*, 45
Spears, Monroe K., *Dionysus and the City*, 49
Spencer, Sharon, 86–87, 140; *Space, Time, and Structure in the Modern Novel*, 140
Spengler, Oswald, 69
Spock, Benjamin, 106
Stapledon, Olaf, 130, 142; *Last and First Men*, 142
Starobinski, Jean, 26
Stein, Gertrude, 31, 43, 79, 86, 103

Steiner, George, 17, 19, 45, 156; *Extraterritorial*, 45; *Language and Silence*, 19, 45
Stern, Daniel, 33, 105; *The Suicide Academy*, 105
Sterne, Laurence, 29, 42, 110; *Tristram Shandy*, 86, 110
Stevens, Wallace, 106, 140, 141
Stockhausen, Karlheinz, 24
Strindberg, Johann August, 20
Sturgeon, Theodore, *More Than Human*, 142, 143
Styron, William, 86, 100, 102; *The Confessions of Nat Turner*, 86, 102
Sukenick, Ronald, 83, 87, 106–107, 141; *The Death of the Novel and Other Stories*, 106, 141–142; *Out*, 141
Swift, Jonathan, *Gulliver's Travels*, 112
Sypher, Wylie, *Literature and Technology*, 49

Tate, Allen, 44, 101
Taylor, Gordon Rattray, 18
Taylor, Peter, 100
Teilhard de Chardin, Pierre, 92, 103, 121, 124, 130, 133, 134, 147n; *Building the Earth*, 121, 147n; *The Future of Man*, 133
Ter Braak, Menno, 26
Thibaudeau, Jean, 56
Thomas, Dylan, 12
Thompson, William Irwin, 79, 126; *At the Edge of History*, 126
Tibetan Book of the Dead, The, 121, 147n
Tinguely, Jean, 21, 53
Todorov, Tzvetan, xiv
Toffler, Alvin, *The Futurists*, 166
Tolstoy, Leo, 44, 158, 159; *Anna Karenina*, 158; *What Is Art?*, 44, 158
Tomkins, Calvin, *The Bride and the Bachelors*, 58
Toynbee, Arnold, 123
Trilling, Lionel, 5, 10, 15n, 44, 48, 51, 156; *Beyond Culture*, 51
Trotsky, Leon, 158–159, 160; *Literature and Revolution*, 158
Troy, William, 90, 92

Ussher, Arland, 83

Valéry, Paul, 31, 41, 43, 48, 140
Verne, Jules, 112

Vico, Giambattista, 63, 69, 78, 90, 132
Vidal, Gore, 57
Vinci, Leonardo da, 50
Vonnegut, Kurt, Jr., 101, 105, 113–114, 142; *Player Piano*, 114; *The Sirens of Titan*, 114; *Slaughterhouse Five*, 114; *Welcome to the Monkey House*, 114

Wagner, Richard, 22
Wallant, Edward Lewis, 101
Warhol, Andy, 24, 55, 107; *A*, 107
Warren, Austin, 10, 44, 101; *Theory of Literature*, 10
Warren, Robert Penn, 100
Watts, Alan, 102
Weaver, Harriet, 79
Weizsäcker, Karl Friedrich von, 125
Wellek, René, 4, 10, 11, 12, 15n, 44; *Concepts of Criticism*, 11, 15n; *Theory of Literature*, 10
Wells, H. G., 79, 112, 113, 166
Welty, Eudora, 100
West, Nathanael, 101
Whitman, Walt, 42, 48
Wiener, Anthony, 166, 167; *The Year 2000*, 167

Wiener, Norbert, 17, 92, 136; *The Human Use of Human Beings*, 136
Wiesel, Elie, 19, 46, 102; *A Beggar in Jerusalem*, 102; *Night*, 19
Wilder, Amos, 162
Wilder, Thornton, 80
Wildman, Eugene, 87
Williams, John A., 101
Wilson, Edmund, 31, 43, 44; *Axel's Castle*, 43
Winters, Yvor, 44
Wittgenstein, Ludwig, xiv, 46, 140
Wolfe, Tom, 56
Woolf, Virginia, 41, 48
Woolsey, John M., 88
Wordsworth, William, 116
Wright, Richard, 101
Writers at Work: The Paris Review Interviews, Third Series, 140
Wurlitzer, Rudolph, 86, 108, 141; *Flats*, 141; *Nog*, 86, 108–109

Yeats, William Butler, 31, 41, 43, 48, 50, 56, 59, 140, 155, 160

Zamyatin, Yevgeny, *We*, 112
Zekowski, Arlene, *Seasons of the Mind*, 106